Arthur Marshall

I SAY!

HAMISH HAMILTON
LONDON

First published in Great Britain 1977
by Hamish Hamilton Ltd
90 Great Russell Street London WC1B 3PT

Copyright © 1976, 1977 by Arthur Marshall

SBN 241 89682 7

Printed in Great Britain by
Western Printing Services Ltd
Bristol

CONTENTS

Acknowledgments	ix
Royal Mail	1
I Liked Ike	5
Panto-time	8
Praise ye the Lord	12
Faites Vos Jeux	15
Only a Suggestion	18
Growing Pains	21
Ichabod	24
Exit Smiling	27
All Beer & Skittles	30
Poles Apart	33
Saints Alive	36
Taking Liberties	39
Heaven Knows	42
Sybil	45
Brace Yourself	48
Fire Down Below	51
Take Me to a Leader	54
Press on Regardless	57
Some Fine Day	60
Modern Luxilife	63
How's That?	66
Bad Language	69
I.T.A.L.Y.	72
Double Dutch	75
Curtain Up	79
Knock Knock	82

Pleased to Meet You	85
On Average	88
Suffer the Little Children	91
Crystal Balls	94
Quiet Flows the Don	97
Down the Red Lane	100
All Wrong on the Night	104
In at the Shallow End	109
Happy Days	112
Off My Chest	116
There Go Your Pips	119

Critic's Corner

Frontal Attack	125
Strawberries and Cream	128
Still a Peasant at Heart	132
Yours Truly	134
Yum Yum	137
Forging a Career	139
Beatie in the Bois	141
Is My Screw Loose?	143
Roll out the Barrel	145
Bramah Rams & Bath Buns	148
Mavis, alias Bungaloosie	150
Where the Nuts Come From	152
A Whole lot of Nothing	155
Battles of Britons	157
Thanks, Yanks	159
Is this a Record?	161
More Good than Harm	164
Absolutely Helpless with Mirth	166
Great Sheik-up	169
She's a Lady	171
Hard Mattresses	174
His Master's Voice	177

TO
PETER KELLAND

ACKNOWLEDGMENTS

The majority of the pieces assembled here were written in 1976 and for the *New Statesman*. I am grateful indeed to the Editor of this distinguished magazine both for his welcome to its pages and its First Person column and for his permission to reprint some of the results. I also thank the Editors of the *Sunday Telegraph* and the *Evening Standard* for similar kindnesses.

ROYAL MAIL

                                      19 Tregunter Crescent, W.8

Your Majesty,

After much hesitation I am taking the liberty of writing to you to ask a favour on behalf of my daughter, Penelope. Young Penny, a well developed 12 year old, has recently 'taken up' tennis and has visions of becoming a second Christine Truman! There are no courts at her Comprehensive, though promised, and she 'makes do' in the park.

On my way to and from work (at the Army and Navy Stores) my bus takes me between Victoria and Hyde Park Corner and past the Palace gardens. These have always intrigued me and from the top of the bus one gets a lovely view. With the leaves off the trees, your hard tennis court becomes very clear. It looks in perfect condition, with everything at the ready and the net up, but I have never seen anyone playing on it. Would it be possible, I wonder, for my Penny to make use of it?

                        Yours sincerely,
                        Pamela Johnston

            From the Lady Jean Sidebotham
                          Buckingham Palace, S.W.1

Dear Mrs Johnston,

Her Majesty has commanded me to answer your letter and to say that she regrets that she does not feel able at the present time to agree to your request.

                        Yours sincerely,
                        Jean Sidebotham
                Lady-in-Waiting to Her Majesty

Dear Lady Sidebotham,

There seems to have been some misunderstanding. I was not

expecting that Her Majesty would be able to play with Penny, she is clearly much too busy. My daughter would bring along one of her friends. Of course, if Her Majesty would care for a knock-up during a slack time in state affairs, that would be a marvellous bonus!

Penny and her friend would bring their own tennis balls. Their best days would be Tuesday or Friday about 2.30 p.m. They are both very excited at the possibility.

Yourse sincerely,
Pamela Johnston

Dear Mrs. Johnston,
   Your further letter has been considered and it is regretted that no exception can be made in this case.

Yours sincerely,
Jean Sidebotham

20 Tregunter Crescent, W.8

Dear Queen,
   My good friend and neighbour, Mrs. Johnston, has been telling me how you are planning to be throwing open your tennis courts to youngsters. This is being great good news. My daughter, Helga, 'caught the tennis bog' while staying with her Onkel Heinrich in Hanover last summer and would also like to 'join up' with the group.

Hullo!
Gertrud Bauscher

Dear Mrs. Bauscher,
   Her Majesty has commanded me to answer your letter and to say that she is sorry that you have been misinformed and that the tennis-court cannot be liberated for public use.

Yours sincerely,
Jean Sidebotham

Dear Lady Sidebotham,
   I understand that Mrs. Bauscher has written—it was foolish of me to let her into our little secret. Of course if you extend the invitation to everybody the court would become impossibly over-

crowded and this is the last thing we want. When would it be convenient for the children to start to play?
>Yours sincerely,
>Pamela Johnston

Dear Mrs. Johnston,
I would very much like to be more helpful but it will be clear to you that the question of security is, in these sad days, of paramount importance and this, if for no other reason, prevents us giving your daughter access to the Palace grounds.
>Yours sincerely,
>Jean Sidebotham

Dear Lady Sidebotham,
You need have no fear about security. Penny knows better than to damage any trees or shrubs in the garden. We have always brought her up to respect other people's property. Did I spot a side-door to the Palace which the children could use? It's in that wall near to where dear old Gorringes used to be. If the children were to use that there would be less chance of outsiders getting to know what was going on. They would be careful to stick to the path once inside the Palace grounds. What about next Friday?
>Yours sincerely,
>Pamela Johnston

Dear Lady Sidebottom,
I am not understanding why Helga's tickets for the court have not come through. Penny Johnston is cock-a-hop all over the Crescent and nothing for Helga! Is this being British Justice?
>Hullo!
>Gertrud Bauscher

Dear Mrs. Bauscher,
I am afraid that you are under a misapprehension. No tickets are being issued to anybody for Her Majesty's hard tennis court. The question of security is, these sad days, of paramount importance.
>Yours sincerely,
>Jean Sidebotham

Dear Lady Sidebottom,
 We Germans are not fearful persons. We mind little of security. A true German is as secure on tennis-court as on battle-field. Helga fears nothing. She has her karate medal and can protect herself.
Hullo!
Gertrud Bauscher

Dear Lady Sidebotham,
 I wonder if you can have received my last letter. The children are 'all set'—and no news! Next week will be half term and an ideal moment for the children's first visit. Please let me know soon.
Yours sincerely,
Pamela Johnston

From the Hon. Mrs. J. C. B. Tynte
Buckingham Palace, S.W.1

Dear Mrs. Johnston,
 Lady Jean is away from duty at the moment with a complete nervous breakdown and in her absence I am dealing with her letters. As the volume of incoming correspondence is always very great, it is not the Palace practice to retain many letters from the public, or our answers to them, and so I am in some doubt about the 'first visit' to which you refer. Could you please explain?
Yours sincerely,
Muriel Tynte
Lady-in-Waiting to Her Majesty

Dear Mrs. Tynte,
 Certainly. My daughter, Penelope, has recently 'taken up' tennis...

I LIKED IKE

The late, alas, Maurice Bowra—and how one misses that ebullient, generous, warm, witty and hilarious fellow—used to insist that there existed a City firm of solicitors called Mann, Rogers and Greaves—the history of the world in a nutshell. Readers of this, our favourite weekly, are no strangers to oddities connected with names, Literary Competitors, ever keen to earn an honest guinea or two, have often pored over the London telephone directories in search of unusual surnames and have come up with plum after plum; Trampleasure, Flabelli, Nockles, Ponking, Pobjee, Butterfant, Kindlisides, Cram and Jelly. And I am not dreaming it when I say that I once saw, on a railway carriage at Waterloo, a notice which said 'This compartment is reserved for Jeremiah Worms, Margaret Thing and Major Cake'.

However, the names that occurred in one's ordinary workaday world were straightforward indeed and I never thought that I would ever come into the orbit of a man called Milton W. Buffington, or that in time I should come to call him, in my friendly way, 'Milt'. He was, of course, American, and it was wartime. 'Then the soldier' says the Bard, describing our seven stages of gradual disintegration, 'full of strange oaths' and, apparently, seeking the bubble reputation even in the cannon's mouth. Neither in character nor in physique was I what could be called a natural soldier and my strange oaths tended to be such things as 'Golly!' and 'Goodness gracious me!'

I do not do *petit point* embroidery but I had heard that the actor, Ernest Thesiger, had got away with this pleasant and decorative pastime in front-line trenches during the Great War (in old age he was once approached by an agitated female fan who gazed into his face and said anxiously, 'Usedn't you to be Ernest Thesiger?'). One wondered a little bit, on being called up, how one was going to fit in. 'It's such a *bother* when people don't fit in' Edith Evans used to say in a splendidly upper-crust voice in a Farjeon sketch.

It was a happy relief to discover that the army was full of people as ill suited to it as I. Quite early on, and on a very dark and cold night in camp near Aldershot, I heard a sentry being sent out to relieve another. The guard-room sergeant barked orders, a rifle was shouldered, and heavy army boots went clonking off to the perimeter fence. And then, out of the blackness, the sentry who was being relieved spoke. 'My dear, thank God you've arrived! I'm frozen, frozen, *frozen*!'

My closest brush with the cannon's mouth came from our own side, what in soccer they call 'own goal'. After a noisy unpleasantness called Dunkirk, I found myself at a barracks in Kent where one morning an officer was required to march a platoon of guardsmen to the butts for rifle practice. They scraped the bottom of the barrel and this seemingly simple task was entrusted to me, then masquerading as a Lieutenant. Off we set. I had no idea whether it was *de rigueur* to march in front or at the back, so I decided on the former and bravely led the way. Before long, a message came from the rear of the platoon requesting me to take rather longer strides but, apart from that, all was cheerful politeness and I quite enjoyed the little stroll.

Soon the butts came into view. I made, as seemed sensible, straight for them and as we drew near I was surprised by what appeared at first to be a welcoming committee—officers waving flags, people shouting and whistles being blown. On I marched, my men, being guardsmen, following unflinchingly. Alas, yes, we had marched, an impressive moving target, down the wrong and lethal end of the butts and right among the flying bullets. An officer, a well-named Major Blood, removed me from the platoon and pointed out my little blunder, rather rudely I thought. Nobody, of course, praised our manly bearing or steadiness under fire, and I wasn't allowed to march the men back again—a petty-minded gesture.

But I soon learnt a way of coping with ratty senior officers. Usually, the higher they went in rank, the friendlier and cuddlier they were (successful and happy, you see), but with those who hadn't quite made it, one remembered Shaw's dictum, 'All men are children in the nursery'. It didn't need much imagination to picture some red-tabbed and fuming Brigadier back in shorts again, with grubby knees and grumpy face, just about to be soundly smacked and sent supperless to bed.

I also, I regret to say, used sometimes, in periods of stress and strain and worry, to look upon the army as a vast girls' school, with dear Miss Alexander as headmistress, and a jolly staff consisting of Gladys Gort, Winifred Wavell and Alice Auchinleck, and with the lacrosse teams doing rather badly until that breezy little Miss Montgomery took over as games mistress. This piece of utter lunacy (apologies to all concerned) helped one to get by.

I defied old Jerry and fought a most courageous war with typewriters and pieces of paper and I wound up at the headquarters of SHAEF, fully Anglo-American ('Hi, Milt!') and under the nicest and most modest general of them all, General Eisenhower, about whom I'm privileged to have a little experience to relate. When the buzz-bombs began, we were at Bushy Park in Twickenham, Surrey. The bombs had started flying over us, and some of them had decided not to go on but to stop and rest awhile. Though many of us, and especially I, were fully expendable, a wholesale annihilation of the headquarters at that particular time would have been a considerable nuisance and a notice went up, signed by General Eisenhower, saying that when the warning siren went, we were all to take cover in the funk-holes provided, and he added, to encourage us, that he himself would be the first to do so.

One morning the warning went off and I duly plunged down into the nearest underground shelter, as instructed. It was fairly dark but I could just make out another officer there. It was General Eisenhower. We were perched on wooden benches. Nobody else came. No doodle-bug arrived. Silence. Peace. We had been there for about five minutes, when the General spoke. Not a long sentence. 'Well,' he said, 'as long as I keep sitting here, they can't ask me to sign anything.' We then heard a bomb approaching. It passed overhead and shortly after, the engine cut out, there was a pause, and then a distant explosion. Again the General spoke. 'You know, every time I say "Oh Lord, keep that engine going", I feel kinda mean.'

A remarkable man, unlike any other. No wonder we won.

PANTO-TIME

A stage-struck child born in 1910 and in Barnes, London, was in luck for just down the road, over that Boat Race suspension bridge, stood the King's Theatre, Hammersmith, where successful West End productions petered out in a profitable fortnight and by the time I was six I had seen *Peter Pan* twice and had played a loud part in Tinker Bell's miraculous resuscitation. Then came two Christmas pantomimes—*Robinson Crusoe* and *Aladdin*. Perversely I rather preferred the Bad Fairy, all cackles and menace and toothless curses, to the simpering Good Fairy, wobbling to and fro on her points. The latter it was who eventually transported us from her Snowflake Bower to The Land of Dreams Come True, which was fine for those whose dreams happened to consist of plumpish air-borne fairies, brightly illuminated flights of stairs (down which the cast came, in strict order of salary) and fountains spouting pink water. My own dreams were rather less sugary.

I looked on the pantomimes with a slightly patronising gaze as by this time I felt myself theatrically to be something of an old hand, having instantly volunteered when our kindergarten was asked to provide an item for a wartime charity concert. Mary White and I recited the Kipling poem, 'Where are you going to, all you big steamers?' Mary, in primrose yellow, supplied the questions and I, in a sailor suit and on behalf of the steamers, supplied the answers. I also supplied an assortment of supposedly nautical gestures to go with them (eyes shaded seawards, hitching of bell bottoms, a lively hornpipe step or two) and I doubt if the Barnes town-hall has ever been treated to a more revolting spectacle. The applause was thunderous and went straight to my head.

But it wasn't allowed to stay there. Children in those days were a good bit repressed—kindly treated, usually, but in no way encouraged to shine. I used to be sent sometimes to a Sunday afternoon church service and when the offertory bag was going round we all sang,

> Hear the pennies dropping!
> Hark, the pennies fall!
> Every one for Jesus,
> He shall have them all.

Well, I thought, this is a rum business! Jesus is in heaven, what on earth does He want with our pennies? And so I piped up with a question along these general lines and got into terrible hot water—'irreligious child, impertinence, how dare you speak?'—and so on. My moment of glory was over.

On our return from the pantomime outings, my parents, keen theatre-goers, were full of happy reminiscence. Some years before, they had been to Drury Lane and had seen Dan Leno, famous both as beanstalk Jack's doting mother (Mrs. Simpson, of all evocative names) and as governess to the Babes in the Wood. There was also the merry occasion when he had appeared with Marie Lloyd, recklessly cast in the title role of *Red Riding Hood*. The director naively thought that it would provide a moving moment if Miss Lloyd, while preparing for bed, knelt and said her prayers. This she duly did but then, being Marie Lloyd, she peered under the bed for a handy object that wasn't there and then prowled round the room in further, frantic search (this moment was subsequently cut). Meanwhile, Dan Leno as the Dame was disrobing in a flurry of red flannel petticoats and whale-bone corsets.

'Where is her equal in tights today?' Godfrey Winn once dramatically asked. He was referring, of course, to Dorothy Ward, one of the best Principal Boys of them all. Nowadays, real young men are more usually pressed into service, most modern children being so knowledgeable ('Mummy, is that big tall lady a lesbian?'). But in their hey-day, slapping those firm thighs, how splendid they were—Clarice Mayne as Jack, Cora Goffin (now Lady Littler) delighting the Midlands year after year, Vesta Tilley as Captain Tralala in *Sinbad*, and to my mind the most remarkable of all, Miss Fay Compton. She was a good old 48 when she last did the Prince in *Cinderella* and an astonishment of youth and grace and precision and firm singing. When I met her, I asked how it was done. 'You must believe every single thing you're doing—the fighting, the love-making, those weird rhyming couplets. If you don't, the children smell a rat at once and you're done for.'

Years ago, on a sunny August day, I was fortunate enough to see Dorothy Ward, looking, as always, just about 16, giving a lunch party at the Ivy Restaurant. Gathered happily together were seven other handsome ladies—pretty summer hats, white gloves—and there was a purposeful air about them all. There was no doubt what it was—a meeting of provincial Principal Boys up in London to choose the songs they were all going to belt out twice daily for twelve weeks from Boxing Day. I somehow felt that it would have been fitting for Miss Ward to greet these great figures in Shakespearean fashion:

'How now, sweet Leeds? Welcome, good Huddersfield! Come, gentle Birmingham and hither, valiant Hull, trill me your ditties awhile!'

Miss Ward is famous too for an act of selfless devotion and heroism. At the final curtain, she used to risk immediate electrocution by getting herself plugged in to an electrical point in the stage and lighting up several coloured bulbs concealed here and there about her person. Our cheers were deafening.

In my childhood I passed the King's Theatre, Hammersmith (next week: Fred Terry in *The Scarlet Pimpernel*) almost every day. No schoolboy ever went to school more willingly and my shining morning face was a sight to behold on the No. 9 bus as it bowled down Castelnau, crossed Hammersmith Broadway, and stopped at Colet Gardens. For there, overlooking what were then St. Paul's School playing-fields, stood the world's least intimidating school—the Froebel Institute.

The Froebel positively bulged with delights. There were Miss Baines and Miss Willis and Miss Champness. In jam-jars there were sticky chestnut-buds that excitingly opened. There was a vast sand-pit and a revolving summer-house. There were steaming roly-poly puddings and, best of all for me, there were endless theatricals. In no time at all I had appeared as one of King Arthur's knights, as a French doctor, and, for reasons which escape me, as a mouse.

There was a pleasing amount of English literature and a surprisingly keen interest in Longfellow's poem, Hiawatha. We recited Hiawatha, we learnt chunks of Hiawatha, we acted Hiawatha. The boys took it in turns to *be* Hiawatha, and when my go came round, the girl allotted to me as my Minnehaha, or Laughing Water, was rather tall and beefy and was called Felicity. She could only be squeezed with difficulty into our communal wigwam. Felicity wore enormous gig-lamps, and when the others, led by Miss Champness, intoned the lines 'And the lovely Laughing Water seemed more lovely as she stood there' it was wiser for me to think of other things. For by this time I had started getting into trouble for Irreverence. I found too many people too comical for words.

In due course a gala Froebel concert was announced, with items supplied both by pupils and grown-ups. After weeks of sickly sucking-up to Miss Champness, I had managed to secure the role of Hiawatha at the concert, saddled though I was with my myopic Minnehaha. For the great day they had obtained a rather more commodious wigwam and while poor old Felicity was blundering her way into it behind the curtain, a largish lady in the full bloom of middle age seated herself at the piano on the front part of the stage and, after warming up the instrument and herself with some elaborate and tuneful bangings, started out on a number new to me, 'There are Fairies at the Bottom of my Garden'. The *chanteuse* did her best with the nauseating affair, but when she came to the line 'Did you know that they could sit upon a moonbeam?' it was too much for me. Apart from anything else, the nursery word for 'bottom' was 'sit-upon'. I lost the little control I ever had. Chuckles, increasing in violence, could be heard from behind the scenes, and heard unfortunately by my mother, seated proudly in the front row, as befitted the fair Wenonah, or Hiawatha's mother.

And alas, the fair Wenonah became extremely angry later and we travelled home in silence. Various privileges were withdrawn (I trembled for my Christmas treat, *Goody Two Shoes*, but we went). I was scowled at. Miss Champness looked *blessée*. Laughing Water took it upon herself to get grumpy. But did, you wonder, this cruel cold-shouldering stop me enjoying ladies defiantly announcing the presence of wee winged visitors? Not yet it hasn't.

PRAISE YE THE LORD

I grieve, though not perhaps very deeply, that the days of Smart Winds are over. Victorian and Edwardian travellers used to be, when abroad and in O.K. places, in a state of permanent excitement about them. There was the Föhn, which created a bother in Northern Italy and Switzerland. There were the Sirocco, that well-known hazard of the Mediterranean, and the Mistral, which can make such a nonsense of the South of France. It has occurred to me that any once popular English resort, temporarily down on its luck, might revive interest in itself by inventing its very own Wind. Bournemouth's could be the dreaded Flatella, a doom-laden breeze which rises, and no man can explain why, in the wooded hills near Tolpuddle and, moving relentlessly South-East, pours itself down the Chines and into the very heart of Bournemouth, engulfing the inhabitants in gloom and despondency. It would provide a talking-point for chic visitors: 'My dear, we were so lucky. The very day we arrived, the Flatella had blown itself right out!'

The thing to do with Winds is to miss them, to be elsewhere, but there was no missing the icy wind that blew, for six months of the year, through the streets and over the playing-fields of Oundle, that jolly and effective school in Northamptonshire, which for beauty of town, village and countryside is one of England's most under-rated counties. Our wind was called, quite simply, the North Wind and it came direct from the Pole. To the North and East of Oundle lay flat fens and the Soke of Peterborough and that gaunt, grim cathedral, all of negligible value as wind jammers. For half the year we shivered and shook.

It would ill become me at this late stage to take a side-swipe at those who in my youth struggled to educate me. Indeed, I have nothing but gratitude for the golden oldies who dispensed history, maths, frog and other necessities. I was not, as has been only too apparent over the last forty years in these pages, scholar material. Frivolous stuff I was. But if I did have a small complaint, it would concern the question of religious observance and instruction.

As in the unforgettable *If* (the film, not the poem), the chapel and the O.T.C. were in the same capable hands (he was known as the Church Militant). Another master in holy orders had himself, in 1939, pluckily, and just for the duration, unfrocked, or whatever, in order to go off and drop bombs on the Germans (and he was known as 'For What You Are About To Receive'). Between the chaplain and the headmaster (I speak of the Twenties and Thirties), a daunting Sunday programme was arranged that nowadays seems almost unbelievable.

Holy Communion (not compulsory) was at 8 a.m. and if you attended it you had to run all the way back to the house to be in time for Morning Prayers at 8.45. We knelt in the dining-room, while the porridge grew cold and sullen before our half-closed eyes, and the General Confession was always included, which took care of any Saturday evening indiscretions. Matins, frequently with sermon, were from 10 to 11, and there was a scripture lesson from 12 to 1. 6 p.m. saw us all at Evensong and often singing 'Abide With Me', known to the wittier boys as the dentists' hymn because of the line 'Change and decay in all around I see'. From 7.30 to 8.30 there was scripture preparation, when we either learnt the Beatitudes by heart or wrote a thoughtful essay on which sin we considered to be the most disastrous (such a *choice*, there was). Then there were House Prayers again, with the General Confession (Sunday afternoon infelicities) and a hymn.

If you wanted further confabs with the Maker, you could say your private prayers on retiring. All this tots up to nearly five hours, and to accomplish it we were attired from head to foot in deepest black. The result? Agnostics by the cartload. Modern schoolboys, grumbling about one compulsory church service a week (the average, I gather) should count their blessings.

One had, of course, to fight back and invent little merry moments for oneself. There were the Chapel Stakes, when we betted on which master would be the first to rise to his feet after the final Blessing. There was fun to be found in the hymns ('Gladly, Thy cross-eyed bear'). There was a complicated cricket game during the headmaster's outstandingly dusty sermons (whenever he removed his glasses, a wicket went down). I managed to make our home-made school Litany tolerable by combining pleasurable thoughts of the holiday treat (always a

theatre matinée) with the relief afforded by ailments, grave or trivial, which got one off work and chapel and into the kindly hands of Matron.
For Jack Buchanan, Cicely Courtneidge and Beatrice Lillie,
    We thank Thee, oh Lord.
For Marie Tempest, Lilian Braithwaite and Binnie Hale,
    We thank Thee, oh Lord.
For Delysia and Yvonne Arnaud,
    Nous Te remercions, Seigneur.
For impetigo, pink eye and German measles,
    We thank Thee, oh Lord.
For broken legs, influenza and the humble chest-cold,
    We thank Thee, oh Lord.
For Miss Wibberley, Miss Pilkington and Miss Buick,
    We thank Thee, oh Lord.
One happy Michaelmas term, the first two Sunday preachers were discovered to be called Wild and Woolly. Little things like that helped.

A chance came to put some of this right. After Cambridge, I returned to Oundle as a master and found myself, at two days' notice, presiding at a scripture lesson. Twenty docile scientists faced me and our 'set book' was the Gospel of St. Matthew. I was panic-stricken as to how to extract lightness and enjoyment from this rather arid material and we spent the first lesson solemnly reading, turn by turn, the text. Alas, it failed to grip. When, on the second Sunday, we started off reading again, I saw despair on every face. It was unbearable. So I stopped the boy who was reading and said 'Oh dear, isn't this dreadful! What *are* we to do?' A polite silence fell.

There had recently been published *Brave New World*. It had caused a stir. We abandoned St. Matthew and we read and discussed Aldous Huxley. Despair disappeared. We then passed on to *The Green Pastures* and acted scenes from it (considerable competition for the role of De Lawd). We read Lytton Strachey. We read H. G. Wells. We read Stella Gibbons. We read anything that wasn't St. Matthew. The Headmaster, a delightful man, heard what was going on but kindly looked the other way. Even the end-of-term exam result (an average of 7 per cent and three boys scoring 0) went by without comment. One doesn't want to take any sort of swipe at a school as understanding as that. Warm-hearted they were, and that North Wind blew in vain.

FAITES VOS JEUX

A pleasant fireside pastime is for those present to choose the one event in the world's rich panorama of memorable happenings that they would most have liked to witness. Give, as the exam papers have it, reasons for your choice. Selection is difficult and the possibilities are varied indeed: Coronation of Elizabeth I, Noah safely afloat, Hardy kissing Nelson, the Last Supper, the Duke of Clarence upside down in that butt of malmsey, the Wright ('Chocks away!') Brothers airborne for the first time, etc.

More interesting to me are some of the minor historical moments featuring slightly less well publicised events. The expression on Wellington's face, for example, when the populace, enraged by his attitude to the Reform Bill, hurled brickbats through the windows of Apsley House on the anniversary of Waterloo (the owner's only known comment was 'Rum day to choose, I *must* say!'). And there was the evening, now remembered by few, when Maynard Keynes, fascinated all his life by the laws of chance and the rules of probability as demonstrated all too clearly and expensively on roulette tables, came bursting into the Cambridge rooms of J. T. Sheppard (subsequently a famous Provost of King's) with an excited shout of 'I hear they've suppressed zero in the Casino at Dieppe.' Sheppard looked up. 'I suppose that means we must cross to France tonight?' 'Of course. Pack at once.'

Non-gamblers will naturally require an explanation of what the suppression of zero entails. I am not an expert but I did learn how to play roulette, though not how to win, at what all must regard as the fountain-head: the Casino at Monte Carlo. Lush Edwardian novels with Riviera settings, together with dramatic silent films (how *yellow* all the participants looked), had warned me what to expect both from gamblers and misers. They were what was known as 'crazed'. Misers gloated in private over their hoards of gold coins, occasionally pouring handfuls of them rather uncomfortably over their heads and shoulders (crazed Lon Chaney was particularly skilled at this). Gamblers, hair on end and eyes starting from their heads, muttered and mouthed at the gaming tables, watched by scornful and elaborately bejewelled *poules de luxe* while they plunged ever more heavily and disastrously.

In these respects the Monte Carlo Casino came as a disappointment. No shouts of despair: no crazed punters: no *poules, de luxe* or otherwise. The croupiers looked like eminent French cabinet ministers who had decided to retire and go into the undertaking business: black suits, white shirts, black ties. The lofty rooms and the dim lighting were churchlike and the hushed voices and general air of dedication reminded one of a religious service. The worshippers at the tables showed no emotion. Triumph or failure, it seemed to be all one. I realised, with some astonishment, that gamblers only want to win in order to be able to continue gambling. The amassing of wealth doesn't come into it. Losing has a mere nuisance value as it removes them, for the time being, from the tables.

The surest way to lose at roulette is to play regularly and to have a system (the proprietors of Casinos have all got A levels in maths). The only way to win any sizeable amount is to risk all on just one spin of the wheel. The odds paid to winning gamblers are based on the assumption that there are 36 numbers. There are not. There are 37, including the dreaded zero. To popularise a resort's Casino by suppressing zero for a week or two (presumably by filling in its little slot and denying it the ball) increases the chance of a win. Hence Keynes's excitement and the midnight Channel crossing.

It was, up to a point, a success story. They each won £40, and in the days when pounds were pounds, but it proved to be the Provost's undoing, though a perfectly happy one. Every vacation thereafter (wars intervening) he made a beeline for Monte Carlo. An impressive spectacle, and never averse to being *en évidence*, he sat at the tables in a sort of dusty fall-out of cigarette ash, biscuit crumbs and white hairs, a wild and storm-tossed King Lear. For him the thrill of gambling lay in actually putting the counters, fifteen at a time when flush, on the table. Frequently, even if he could have chosen the number to come up he would have won nothing. He betted against himself.

From time to time he ran out of money and one had, if near at hand, to lend him more ('Bless you, dear boy!'). Sometimes he was found, quite innocently, attempting to remove somebody else's winnings ('*Pardon!*') and there was a momentary unease at the table. No race can sniff as disapprovingly as the frogs. Occasionally the injustice of the world in general and of casinos in particular would overwhelm him. The years of study devoted to becoming a distinguished Greek scholar had left little time for other languages and he had to manage as best he could, exiting from the building with a loud cry of '*Maisong de voleurs!*'

As the Cambridge term approached, his gambling friends had to remind him of the date, then to pack his things (heavy woollen underwear, flannel shirts, starched butterfly collars, serviceable black boots) and then to get him, loudly protesting, to the Monte Carlo station and push him into the train. The first attempt at getting him back to King's always failed. His conscience, we must assume, struggled with the gambling urge but lost the brief battle. At Nice the Provost would alight, speedily change platforms and come blithely winging back to Monte Carlo on the next available train, chuckling loudly at this irresponsible and juvenile prank.

Freud who, if really pushed, could find sexual significance in a spoonful of cold mashed potato, unearthed all sorts of concealed sublimations in gambling—the flutter of hands dealing cards (masturbation), the pushing to and fro of the croupier's rake (copulation), the rattle of dice in a box and the click of the ball in the wheel (assorted aberrations). It is true that Dostoevski, a life-long roulette buff, reported to his wife that he experienced sexual stimulation when *losing* large sums, a treat not hard to come by. And it is always said that devoted gamblers make, when in the home, listless lovers.

None of this stuff applied to the Provost. He was a character in a Greek tragedy, pitting himself, knowing he would lose, against the Fates, those dreary spinning ladies who so seldom spin anything remotely pleasant. The certainty of failure was somehow reassuring and in no way lessened the feeling of painful excitement, a feeling, come to think of it, not unlike that experienced when falling in love. Perhaps Freud was right after all.

ONLY A SUGGESTION

Posterity, which may have it in for us for our completely irresponsible squandering of oil and petrol (and when they run out, what else is going to be able to heave aeroplanes into the air in such vast numbers?), may well bless us in other, rather minor, ways. The bound copies of *Punch*, for example, provide an invaluable source and pictorial record of pastimes, fashion, attitudes, games, social life, politics and the arts. And what made us, or didn't make us, laugh.

If Posterity ever gets its hands on the Suggestion Books of a famous London Club it will find there a record of gluttony, privilege, arrogance, selfishness and bad temper that will set future historians ferreting about for accounts of revolutions and uprisings that miraculously never occurred. One such book happens to have come my way—no names, no pack drill: and no requests for resignation either.

The suggestions are enormously varied. We range from a request to the librarian for regular deliveries of the 'Calcutta Daily News' and the 'Allahabad Pioneer', and a demand that all drinking water should be passed through a Pasteur filter (on the way *in*, that is), to a request that Bengalese Hash be served at luncheon, which excitingly sparks off greedy screams for Hungarian goulash, Austrian paprika chicken, Vienna steaks, and a large wall map of the Balkans to be hung in the hall (1912, and not a moment too soon).

Sometimes the pace quickens and we hardly know where we are: more 'cigar rests' in the lavatories, an extra curry cook, all newspapers to be ironed and then the pages sewn together along the fold, stronger lemon in the barley water, noisy tea-drinkers to be 'spoken to', cancel the *Journal Amusant* ('objectionable matter and offensive illustrations'), penholders to be washed daily, the 'entirely unsuccessful portrait of the late Prime Minister' to be removed, the wind indicator to be repaired, more interesting fruit ('Why no nectarines?'), patriotism ('M*u*st we buy foreign cigar-cutters?'), 'our absurdly small wine list contains only 23 choices of champagne', and in 1914 a request for the *New Statesman* ('It has much valuable information').

Two subjects are commented on repeatedly and at great length and are found to be especially agitating: ventilation and fish. Should the morning-room windows be opened for 10 minutes every hour ('*not* during cold weather' pleads a wobbly fist) to expel 'exhausted air'. Will the new ventilators in the coffee room put paid to disagreeable smells from the drains or merely chill the food? Why not these newfangled electric fans everywhere? Can gentlemen flap hand-fans and remain manly? How injurious are draughts? Is a violent rush of wind through the hall desirable when ladies, even though rarely, are present? Should they be warned to expect it (''ware wind!')? Could rooms be safely ventilated at night and windows thrown open in 1917 or would the merest chink of light cause Count Zeppelin himself, hovering above, instantly to flatten the building with one of his devilish 50-pounders?

Fish, being food, is even more passionately discussed. We start with a *poissoniste* putting forward a strong argument for 'a daily choice of the only possible fish, by which I mean turbot, sole or plaice and *not* mackerel or herrings.' Nobody dreams of sullying the pages with the word 'cod'. 'Can't we have more red mullet?' slobbers a red mullet-lover. But not too much of it ('Red mullet *again*', we read). We mark time with an argument on the desirability or otherwise of bloaters, with a wistful sideways glance at sprats, scallops and smelts and, of all things, a demand for *bouillabaisse* (for those with no French, say it BOO-EEE-YAH-BASE). And then, and the *shame* of it, a page torn out and a stern comment: 'The Committee regret that there is a Member of the Club who requires to be reminded that this book is not to be used for anonymous or objectionable remarks.' Red mullet once more, who can doubt it?

Not all, unfortunately, is merry and some of the entries, even across so many years, sicken one. The Club's closing hour (2 a.m.) seems inhuman, and prompt service was insisted on. 'Sandwiches should not take *ten minutes* to prepare at 11.30 in the evening' —and this from kind Robert Ross, with not even the excuse of Oscar (dead by now) keeping him up late. On Poppy Day there had been 'unseemly conduct by flag-sellers, so let them remain *outside* the vestibule' and in the cold. 'I hope that the closing of the Club for Christmas may not be taken as a precedent' and that the 100 servants involved should not enjoy themselves too. And perhaps the most depressing of all, a request that the police should not allow out-of-work ex-servicemen, trying to earn a bob or two by playing musical instruments in the streets, to 'plant themselves in Pall Mall'—'hideous cacophony of unmusical sounds' etc. etc.

Very occasionally the outline of a complete life presents itself. One turns a page and an aroma of strong waters from the past is almost sniffable. And there, amid some brownish stains and in a handwriting that would score 0 out of 10 even in a kindergarten, we find our subject's first entry. 'March 24th. I do not like the Brandy served in the Club.' Silence for a day, while he tests it again to make quite quite sure, and then (0 out of 10 for spelling, too), 'March 26th. Formely we head some good Brandies supplied but not like the prescent.' Six weeks go by (Out of town? In a home?) and then he strikes again. 'May 10th. I do not like the Brandies served here.'

We think we have lost him, but no. Five months later and back he comes. 'Why not a change of Brandy?' And then, surprisingly, he branches out. 'There is a lack of want of suppervision here of many things' and 'Can nothing be done to catch the flies in the rooms?' No, nor the flying pink elephants either. Five days later there is, and here he shows his finer side, a reference to the nutritional value of Jerusalem artichokes, but then alas it's back to the old theme with a last despairing plea in a forest of blots through which one can just make out the magic word. And that is that.

But no, not quite. Three long years pass and then suddenly—it is Springtime—he pops up again. Only a few words. 'April 19th. Why not more tasty pastries?' Not a whiff of brandy. No smudges. Handwriting firm, spelling quite faultless. Just a suggestion for wholesome and appetising food. This member at least has slain the Demon Drink and been finally purified. Reformed, in fact.

GROWING PAINS

Life's Whirligig has brought me quite often into happy contact and friendship with the rich—the rich with ordinary names like you and me, and the rich whose names are redolent of wealth and brimful with solid, financial promise. I have found both sorts invariably kind and generous but I do not, I tell myself, envy them. They tend to arrange for themselves agitating lives, not helped by their inability to stay in the same place for very long. They suffer from a malaise which one might call Rich Fidgets. They have too much energy. The rest of us, exhausted from battling in and out of Sainsbury's, ask nothing better than to sit down quite quietly somewhere and stare at the wall.

And in addition to buzzing too vigorously about, the rich have another hobby of which they are probably unaware. I refer to Tumbril Talk, the uttering of sentences that will not be out of place as they rattle over the cobbles and the heads begin to roll. For example, I gave a rich friend a lift in my car. I was rather proud of it—a Ford Consul, Goodwood green and freshly washed. He looked, as he saw it, envious, and indeed he was. 'You're so *lucky* to have a cheap car. They never get stolen.' And there was Lady Juliet Duff, an exceptionally agreeable person and with access to great possessions, who was commiserating one day with a far from affluent friend who was hard up. 'Oh, but there's really no problem', she said, 'just sell *all* your Fabergé.'

Rich Fidgets can be productive of stressful atmospheres but I was no stranger to such things. I had grown up with them. My father, though a kindly disposed man, was one of those who can effortlessly create about them Pools of Unease. Experiencing, in public, a momentary gêne, a boredom, an anxiety, he was wishful to share the unwelcome feeling with those about him. The theatre, if the play was a dud, found him operating freely and the tools of his trade were ready to hand—clearings of the throat, yawns, deep sighs, hurried glances to right and left, shiftings and shufflings, windings of watches. The pool widened and widened.

In the enclosed space of a railway carriage compartment, my father was to be seen at his best. Expansive, he became. He enjoyed talking, and especially to unknowns. It was easy enough to set conversational balls in motion: 'Do you realise that we are now only eight miles from Slough?' or 'Which are your favourite pianola rolls?'. Here, though there were no Pools of Unease, another hazard hovered—my father's confidence that he was a dab hand at spotting an accent, a confidence which, despite frequent huffy rebuffs, never weakened. 'Exactly which district of Newcastle do you come from?' 'But... I don't understand... Newcastle? I've never even been there.'

Once we nearly got into fisticuff trouble. It was 1940 and we were travelling to London. 'When were you last in Cork?' my father demanded of a rather sullen male fellow-passenger who had only with difficulty been nudged into chat ('What baccy's that you're smoking?'). It was wartime. Eire was neutral. The question carried a hint of something not quite right: of spying, perhaps, or some such underhand stuff. The man, who had, as he later revealed, spent his entire life in Ealing, became belligerent. Even my father was silenced.

But not all was unease and belligerence. One day he returned to our Sunday lunch in a state of great exaltation. He had been to our Barnes garage to prepare the car, a stately Metalergique, for an afternoon picnic outing. Our picnics were often to a place which I have since been unable to locate. It was called Loudwater. There was certainly water but I do not remember it as being especially loud. The name had somehow a sort of indecency about it, a hint of somebody doing No. 1 to a background of explosions (in the nursery the bodily functions were known as No. 1 and No. 2, the fact that there would, in due course and in God's good time, be a No. 3 being prudently withheld from me. No point in facing up to this distasteful complication sooner than necessary).

It appears that my father, returning from the garage along Castelnau, the wide road which joins Barnes to Hammersmith, had seen, bowling sedately towards him, a large black car with no number plate. This could only mean one thing, Royalty, and indeed within the car were to be seen King George V and Queen Mary, bound who knows whither. My father swept off his hat and bowed. The King and Queen politely inclined their heads. The car bowled on.

As we munched our lunch, my father mused awhile on what would have happened if, say, he had suddenly fainted dead away with the excitement. Would the car have stopped? Would Queen Mary have pressed forward with smelling-salts? Would they have driven him home (all of eighty yards)? Would my mother have come rushing out, curtseying? I longed, irreverent as ever, to ask what would have happened if, more interestingly, my father's braces had suddenly burst and his trousers had fallen down to his ankles. Clapped in the Tower? Executed on the spot? Would Queen Mary have fainted? But I had learnt not to voice such thoughts.

I had not always been so careful. I had started reading at a relatively early age and all was grist to my mill. When we stayed with my Ilfracombe grandparents, acceptable (to me) reading matter was hard to come by. My grandfather was a devout clergyman and the books in his study tended to be collections of sermons (Canon Bellamy had been woefully prolific and a regular Rev Gasbag of the pulpit) or were concerned with St. Paul's interminable journeys. Wandering into the kitchen one Sunday, I found and made off with the cook's newspaper and, settling down for a good read, found myself at once in the middle of a puzzlement.

A Judge, it seemed, had been extremely ratty with, and had given a five year sentence to, some man who, in a public park, had 'Exposed his person'. Now to me a person was somebody unknown ('Who's that person?'). Exposing I connected vaguely with photography—hypo baths and all that. *His* person implied somebody close to him: an aunt, perhaps. In those days, photography out of doors was unthinkable unless the sun was brightly shining. Five years in jug for coaxing an aunt outside on a balmy day? It didn't seem right, and in a gap in the conversation at tea I raised the subject. It took me some time to get my little message through and, when I did, it was not popular. My total innocence saved me but did not lessen the head-waggings and sorrowful looks. I was, needless to say, given no credit for having attempted to get justice, as I saw it, done.

ICHABOD

It saddens me slightly that the first precaution I now take on entering a theatre to see a new play is to look about for the nearest emergency exit. And not in case of fire, either. I am old and must be forgiven for being, theatrically, set in my ways. It is doubtless entirely my fault that I do not always understand what is unfolding before me and, not understanding, become restless. I greatly enjoyed No Man's Land and the superb performances of John Gielgud and Ralph Richardson. Wishful to discover afterwards what on earth the plot could have been about, I questioned Sir John, an old friend. He himself did not seem entirely sure. 'I think it's about *menace*,' he said. 'Oh I see,' I answered in my courteous way.

I haven't done all that amount of plunging headlong out of theatres in mid-performance, but I do now always buy a gangway seat and secure my line of retreat. I first plunged out in 1931, anxious to see no more of a Strindberg piece called The Spook Sonata, which, in conditions of really advanced gloom, featured a Milkmaid, a Consul (not a car) and a Mummy (not a mother), all in ghost form and jabbering away like anything. I do hope things turned out well for them. I plunged once, and with, I'm sorry to say, some rather noisy clangings at the door, out of a sad musical at Drury Lane: somebody was singing a song called 'I'm in love with an octopus'. I plunged bravely ('Sh! Sh!') from The Caretaker when they asked that tramp, just once too often for me, what his name was. And I plunged quickest of all (after two minutes) out of a play called Season of Goodwill (a three week disaster at the Queen's in 1964). I had, as it happens, written it myself and, disloyally first off the sinking ship, found the dialogue boring, long before critics and audiences came sensibly to the same conclusion.

It is, to say the least of it, a sobering experience to be responsible for an expensive theatrical failure. You feel guilty, and indeed you are. Your idea, your characters, your words. A cast (charming and kind throughout) whose time you have wasted and who will shortly be out of a job. Being guilty, you must be punished. The painful lacerations come at regular intervals. The morning press ('This tedious piece...'). The evening papers ('Whatever can have induced H. M. Tennent to...'). The weeklies ('An unhappy evening...'). Highbrow theatre magazines ('We draw a veil...'). Broadcasting critics ('How I kept awake, I shall never...'). And so on and so forth. Even friends (some of them) look at you reprovingly. The author puts a courageous face on things and, walking up Shaftesbury Avenue, I looked so determinedly blithe, sunny and carefree that acquaintances, rightly appalled by the lunatic sight that I presented, shuddered and darted up side streets to avoid me.

A dear, but somewhat caustic, actress, Irene Browne, lived near me. 'How can you be so *brave* after such a fiasco?' she kept saying. She did not visibly get me down and so, deciding she was letting me off too lightly, she changed her tune. 'How can you be so *bold*...?' How indeed? It was a mixture of despair and wounded vanity, laced with bravado. Round about Christmas time, dramatic critics usually give a round-up of the year's offerings, from the peaks to the abysses, and there I was again ('Among the more depressing evenings...'). The end? Not at all. Four years later, a biography of your leading lady is published ('How she can ever have been persuaded...').

I consoled myself then, as I console myself now, by remembering the dear, dead, pre-war matinée days when, as like as not, you went to the theatre to see a star performer rather than to see a particular play. The pieces were referred to as 'an amusing vehicle', written either for somebody like Lilian Braithwaite or for that delicious roly-poly and gurgling frog, Yvonne Arnaud, and are now generally despised and disparaged. Well, they gave great pleasure to many.

I went constantly. With tea in the interval safely ordered (paste sandwiches, Earl Grey, madeira cake), one took a quick glance at the programme's grateful acknowledgements, which delightfully revealed the kind of upper-crust world we were going to move in. Cigarettes by Abdulla. Silverware by Asprey. Furs by Hartnell. Champagne by Moët & Chandon. Jewellery by the Burma Co. Baby grand by Chappell. And finally, a telephone, 'lent by the G.P.O.' Mean, even then.

In the orchestra pit, a sextet, led by a pince-nezed violinist, scrapes its way carefully through gems from Wilfred Sanderson ('Friend o' Mine', etc), the lights lower and the curtain rises on a sumptuous London drawing-room, costly flowers everywhere. Into this bower there enters a trim, uniformed housemaid followed by one of those totally reliable actresses (Martita Hunt, Marda Vanne) in which we have always specialised, fourth on the billing outside the theatre and now playing a totally reliable friend to the female star and called something like Grace Forster. They speak. 'Is her Ladyship not back yet, Saunders?' 'No, Madam. She telephoned from Harrods to say that she had been delayed.' There now! We're probably somewhere in S.W.1, and very nice too. The star's stage husband, grey-haired, distinguished, enters now from downstage right (his study). 'Ah, Grace my dear! *He kisses her.* Stella's expecting you for tea. Any idea what she's up to? She's been looking very *odd* these last few days and all morning she was like a cat on hot bricks.' You see? Excitement, interest, suspense are instantly created. No, Grace has no idea. Nor has Saunders, who has exited.

A car is heard stopping. The front door slams noisily. There is an anticipatory rustle in the audience. Marie Tempest's unmistakable voice is heard, off, probably loading parcels onto Saunders. We provide applause (and if we're sluggish with it, Miss Tempest always started it herself in the wings), the door flies open and in she sails ('Ah, Grace my dear!' *She kisses her*), a pink vision with a saucy hat and twinkling eyes, and off we go for two hours of harmless enjoyment.

In the interval a woman behind me says 'Wonderful, and she must be all of 84'. Bosh, of course, but remarks overheard in the theatre can be profitable. For John Barrymore's *Hamlet*, I sat in front of two smartly dressed middle-aged ladies who were evidently, from their chat, seeing the play for the first time. Fay Compton was Ophelia and went, in due course, quite splendidly mad, gibbering dottily all over the stage. There was a sigh from behind. 'Oh *dear*', said a voice, 'I'm afraid she's going to be tiresome.'

EXIT SMILING

Students of the theatre, and in particular students of dramatists' actual texts, must often have wondered at the varying extent to which playwrights consider it important to guide their actors with helpful indications as to how their lines should be said, coupled with the provision of bits of stage 'business' which the director may or may not use. Some authors provide rather too much guidance, and some rather too little.

One of the former, and at this late stage the criticism will hardly damage his rightly splendid reputation, is Priestley. Never having acted professionally himself, he possibly felt that actors welcome having every indication of mood spelt out for them. In *Dangerous Corner* the dialogue is thickly strewn with explanatory adverbs snugly bracketed: playfully, harshly, sardonically, grimly, sharply, thoughtfully, coldly, briskly, wearily, excitedly, bravely, urgently, mockingly, steadily, emphatically, significantly, and so on, with over 150 in all and including 'half screaming' and 'making a face', which is doubtless what reputable, experienced, resentful actors with ideas of their own would by now be doing.

In *The Sacred Flame*, a similar sort of play with its startling revelations within a close-knit circle, Maugham, very much not an actor either, is more tactful. There is an occasional 'listlessly', 'sullenly', 'kindly' and 'shyly', but on the whole he leaves the performers to get on with it as best they may. And Galsworthy too, in *Loyalties*, knows when to intrude and when to keep mum. Shaw, in all his plays, behaves impeccably to actors, but then he was one himself, of a sort.

For self-indulgence in this field, Barrie would be hard to beat. The pages drip, alas, with his slobbery enjoyments. But he can be disarmingly honest. During one of the first rehearsals of *Peter Pan* in 1904, he tells us, he became aware of an overalled theatre employee standing at his side in the stalls, gloomily watching what was going on (Wendy sewing on Peter's shadow). Eventually he heaved a sigh, turned to Barrie and said glumly, 'The Gallery won't stand this, you know'. For this one can forgive Barrie much, and there is indeed much to forgive.

It was just as well that some of the stage directions were not read out to the Gods. When, in that top-floor nursery, Mr. Darling is trying to cajole Nana, the canine nanny, she 'plays rub-a-dub with her paws, which is how a dog blushes'. Meanwhile Michael is in bed 'doing idiotic things with a teddy-bear', while Wendy enlivens her other brother, John, 'by playing rum-tum on him in bed', these activities being watched by Mrs. Darling, 'the loveliest lady in Bloomsbury', about to 'tidy up the children's minds as if they were drawers', light the nightlights and exit gracefully with a tuneful lullaby.

In the theatre, the play works like magic, despite the perilous moments. Among the friendly redskins we find Tiger Lily, 'the belle of the Piccaninny tribe' ('Scalp um, oho, velly quick'), and her braves ('Ugh, ugh, wah'). There are mermaids ('going plop-plop'). The Never Land boys drink, we are told, 'calabashes of poe-poe' and Nibs sneaks on Slightly ('He hasn't drunk his poe-poe'). Wendy, wanting a kiss, 'holds out her mouth to Peter', not sure whether she is his wife, mother or sister (ugh, ugh). Later on, she tries again: 'Oh, Peter, how I wish I could take you up and squdge you! *He draws back*'. And there is a memorable moment when Wendy explains to her mother about fairies: 'The mauve fairies are boys and the white ones are girls and there are some colours who don't know *what* they are.' Well I never.

Ibsen often supplies, when it matters most, the really telling stage direction. The curtain has not been up two seconds on the first scene of A Doll's House (*Et dukkehjem* in the original) when Nora ('Slam that door!') Helmer comes in, fresh from a shopping expedition. 'Nora enters smiling. She continues smiling in quiet glee, takes from her pocket a bag of macaroons and eats one or two', every inch the healthy, hungry, open, extrovert, **early women's-libber**. And when, in *Ghosts* (*Gengangere*), the Alving orphanage catches fire at the end of Act II (such a challenge for the stage-manager), saintly Pastor Manders, first showing his practical, Norwegian side, utters the immortal line 'and not insured either!' Then, Ibsen tells us, he 'clasps his hands', **either invoking immediate fire-fighting aid from Above in the shape of a sharp shower, or in silent prayer that diseased Oswald** has, during one of his increasingly few lucid moments, been inspired to take out an All Risks policy with the Prudential, the risks to include the likelihood of being poisoned by his mother. No such luck, however (the policy, I mean).

Apart from the well-known and mysterious 'Exit, pursued by a bear', Shakespeare deals only in absolute essentials. It was clearly quite enough trouble to get the actual spoken words down on probably indifferent parchment with a scratchy quill without bothering about mere frills. During the closet scene, Gertrude was almost certainly applying soothing skin creams to neck and shoulders and dabbing on anti-wrinkle unguents where they would do most good, while Hamlet moodily kicked at logs in the fireplace, ruining his sandals, but we have to guess at these things. Just that little bit extra and our understanding of, for example, the home life of the Macbeths would benefit enormously.

Take that 'night to remember' at Inverness. Duncan had, we know, 'supp'd', possibly on smoked salmon, roast venison, an open medlar tart and *les fromages*, and was now, for the time being anyway, safely tucked up and in dreamland. We can assume that his hostess, her mind elsewhere, had merely pecked at her food. Who can doubt that at some point Lady Macbeth indulged in a light but sustaining snack to help her through the rest of what was going to be an unusually busy evening?

> *Lady Macbeth enters hurriedly bearing a heaped platter of baps. With feverish haste, she butters them, spreads them liberally with wild honey, and falls to voraciously.*
> Lady M: *(her mouth full)*. Wog ter ish?
> Macbeth: *(crossly)*. I cannot *hear* you, Elspeth.
> Lady M: I said, what time is it?
> Macbeth: That's better. Twenty past ten.
> Lady M: Remind me to congratulate Maggie in the morning. These baps are tip-top.
> *Lady Macbeth finishes the last one, licks her fingers with a little sigh of repletion and adjusts her whimple.*

You see? Just a few additions and at once we get a fuller, rounder, more human picture of what is, after all, just an ordinary, everyday Scottish family.

ALL BEER & SKITTLES

For some years now it has been extremely unfashionable to be happy. Novels, plays and poems have reflected this and gloom, and not without some cause, is the popular thing. Happiness reveals a frivolous state of mind and the world looks askance and suspiciously at smiling faces (poor disgraced Nixon's courageous attempts at a rueful grin were considered particularly devilish). If you were to walk down Oxford Street smiling and calling a cheerful 'Hullo' or 'Good morning' to passers-by, you would be instantly arrested by the police and subsequently prosecuted, either for soliciting for immoral purposes or for using 'insulting behaviour', with a stiff spell in choky to follow, the Judge sternly announcing 'how intolerable it is when private and seemly persons cannot go about their daily business without being exposed to suggestive, impertinent and evil overtures'.

But not so in Devon. Here at 'Myrtlebank', when we sight our agreeable neighbours at 'Dunroamin'', or any other cheerful village residents, it's loud hullos and good mornings all round and on until the cows come home, when it changes to good evenings instead. All is politeness and friendliness. Beauty and peace are everywhere. In April we are deafened by birdsong, and when the daffs are over there are the primroses to dazzle and delight, such obliging and hardy flowers and at their most contented when out of the sun and facing north. Every morning on waking I count my blessings. I get to 374 and then I stop, fearful that, unless I shut up, the Lord will strike me down.

I have to tell you something. I cannot help being happy. I've struggled against it, but no good. Apart from an odd five minutes here and there, I have been happy all my life. There is, I am well aware, no virtue whatever in this. It results from a combination of heredity, health, good fortune and shallow intellect. It is, in fact, rather a non-virtue as it is apt to bring with it complacency and self-satisfaction. It gives little joy to others. My smiles and beams and chuckles irritate more than they please. But there it is. I love life. Forgive me.

Laughter has much to do with it. The glum mystify me. For many months in the army I worked cheek by jowl with a morose, moustached Major. He disapproved of me deeply, and understandably. I looked a very non-military figure and I took so little seriously. He arrived one day gloomier than ever. 'I say, most other people in the headquarters seem to be using Christian names, so I suppose we'd better start. What's yours?' I have three initials and the first of them is 'C'. 'Cynthia', I answered, trying to lighten the occasion. '*Cynthia?*' 'Yes.' 'That's a bloody silly name for a man.' 'Yes, isn't it?' I said. For some days he called me Cynthia loudly and defiantly until I had to beg him to stop. 'People', I explained, 'are talking', but the feeble fun passed him by.

I learnt laughter at my mother's knee, and with some difficulty for it shook continually. She was as uncontrollable as I was. It wasn't formal 'jokes' that amused us but the way people behaved, the things they said. There was a Torquay restaurant where we sometimes lunched and on one occasion the service had gone badly to pieces. Everybody was having to wait rather long and some were being landed with dishes which they hadn't ordered. Near us were two middle-aged ladies of generous proportions who were without their food and were getting increasingly agitated. At last, one of them plucked up courage and we heard an agonised shout. 'Waitress! Waitress! We're the two stuffed marrows.'

In youth the learning of French could be perilously laughter-provoking, with masters reciting '*Maître corbeau, sur un arbre perché*' and making like a crow. Before going up to Cambridge, I lived with a French family at Grenoble, amid pleasant snow-topped mountains. The family consisted of three unmarried sisters. Sisters that come in threes—Brontës, Chekhov's and Macbeth's—are often weird indeed. There was Mademoiselle Alice, permanently bedridden but registering her presence with little wails and moans and whimpers from a downstairs bedroom. There was Mademoiselle Cécile, the hinterland of whose mouth contained an apparently inexhaustible supply of molars, so frequently was she *chez le dentiste* having extractions, after which she would sit at meal-times clutching her jaw and swaying to and fro, muttering '*Ah, que je souffre!*' Politeness called for some sort of show of sympathy but at that time my limited French could provide nothing more soothing than 'Ah, *pauvre Mademoiselle!*'

The third sister, Mademoiselle Berthe, made up for the two others by being almost excessively robust. She was a fine trencherwoman and her appetite was enormous. It was my first experience of sitting next to a really hungry French lady eating oil-soused lettuce in quite formidable quantities. Her method was to prong a vast forkful, apply it to her mouth and leave the rest to suction, helping a few outlying leaves in with the finger-tips, daintly crooked. The din was tremendous. She was like some machine in a factory, taking in the basic materials and then disgorging ... well, what? In Mademoiselle Berthe's case, the end products were heavy French sighs, ear-splitting eructations, and other manifestations of repletion that I really don't care to go into. To restrain laughter, I had to think firmly of death (*la mort*).

I get quite a lot of simple happiness from running over in my mind activities which the world might consider smart, interesting or enjoyable and in which, thank God, I am *not* taking part. For example, I am not, in drenching rain and an east wind, attempting to light my very own barbecue on my chic little patio in S.W.1. I am not, Kwelled to the eyebrows, fighting *mal de mer* and other nauseas on a Greek ship-owner's luxi-yacht in a choppy Mediterranean. I am not at a 'working lunch', in a tornado of nervous burps and hiccoughs, with the Prime Minister. I am not miles high in Concorde, eating (see advertisements) fois (*sic*) gras, scampi, and 'salad palm hearts specially flown from the Seychelles', a journey which must surely rank as the most lunatic mission of all time. I am not in Singapore and at a 100-course Imperial Chinese banquet (see news item), lasting four days, costing £1,000 a head, and including such *bonnes bouches* as crane soup, fried bears' paws, snake, and antelope's genitalia ('Might I possibly trouble you for the mustard?').

In *The Sound of Music*, melodious Julie Andrews made mention of some of her favourite things, listing among them 'snow-flakes on kittens'. Well, I can rub along without *them*, but the message comes through all right. It's the simple things that, in the end, most cheer the heart. The countryside in all seasons. The wind in the willows. Cowslip fields. Friends. Love. Laughter. The best things in life are, indeed, free.

POLES APART

'Prayed for help and got up earlier'. This, which should perhaps be the wholesome daily practice of all of us, was the prudent step taken by Queen Victoria ('I felt bewildered') on the day in 1863 when she travelled from Balmoral to Aberdeen to unveil a statue ('Oh! It was too painful, too dreadful!') of the fairly recently dead Prince Albert. The reluctant widow, wallowing in her grief, confided all, as usual, to her diary, selected portions of which were later published by wily Smith, Elder & Co. and made available to the public in a hardback called *More Leaves from the Journal of A Life in the Highlands*, a follow-on volume to *Our Life in the Highlands*, which had prominently featured the Prince Consort, then alive and kicking.

Both books sold extremely well. Hot cakes wasn't in it, but one wonders what chance the authoress would have stood had she been an unknown writer submitting her manuscript to a publisher for judgement. How might the publisher's reader's report have gone?

'This garrulous effusion, peppered with exclamation marks, is remarkable only for its egocentricity and has little to recommend it. The account of the opening of the Aberdeen water works lacks bite ('It was very pretty to see the water rushing up'), likewise the visits to a slate quarry and the Ben Nevis Distillery. For the rest, in between the numerous anniversaries of deaths ('No joy! All dead!'), it is the usual stuff and traffic of life in Hoot Toot Land with its annoyances ('The midges are dreadful!'), its breakfasts ('Such splendid cream and butter!'), its heather ('So beautifully pink!'), its disappointments ('No pudding! No fun!'), and its moments of generosity and largesse ('I gave Brown an oxidised silver biscuit-box, and Beatrice an enamelled photograph of our dear Mausoleum').' Brown's comment, incidentally, was 'It is too much', a phrase which offers two interpretations.

Who can doubt that the amateur royal scribblings would

have been promptly turned down? Recently in these pages I said that Mr. Priestley had never acted professionally and I was kindly corrected by a correspondent. He did once appear, it seems, in a play of his own in London. But this merely underlines his strictly amateur status. The gulf between the amateur and the professional is as unbridgeable as the Atlantic ocean. There are few activities more depressing to watch than the spectacle of high-spirited and well-meaning amateur actors letting off steam in, say, a Noël Coward comedy. The clothes, the intonations, the timing, the faces—all, all is wrong. It is a wince a minute. They, of course, are having the whale of a time and it is sad but true that if an actor, or orator, or preacher, or after-dinner speaker is enjoying himself, nobody else is.

The amateur writer reveals himself as speedily as anybody. Some years ago, I was lucky enough to find a pleasant literary niche, reading television plays for H. M. Tennent, who at that time were providing a fortnightly dramatic offering for ITV. For five years I read on an average thirty plays a week, unsolicited plays sent in on spec by hopeful writers. If my mathematics are not too rusty, that means that I read about eight thousand plays (it seemed more). Of these endless plays, only five were any good and they, it turned out, were from professional writers. One soon learnt the danger signs: 'To the right of the cocktail cabinet...': 'To the left of the french windows...': *'Cynthia drops him a mock curtsey.* Thank you, kind sir.' Some of the aspirants had mugged up technical jargon from handbooks ('Camera pans and favours Ethel'). My heart bled for them and I turned them down, by letter, as kindly as I knew how, but we were in a hard, competitive, commercial world and their work was just no good. Where then, did the plays come from? Chiefly from commissioned work from professional TV dramatists. What, then, makes a TV dramatist? Talent and patience and talent and industry and talent and knack and a good bit of luck.

Among the hopefuls there were, of course, a number of charming eccentrics, particularly a delightful gentleman called Harry H. Wimbley. Harry H. Wimbley always wrote on elaborately printed writing paper which bore a large heading saying HARRY H. WIMBLEY PLAY PRODUCTIONS LTD. PRESIDENT—HARRY H. WIMBLEY. The letter then began 'Dear Mr. Marshall, I have pleasure in forwarding the latest comedy by Harry H. Wimbley'. Then the signature was printed, Harry H.

Wimbley and over it, Harry H. Wimbley had signed his name, Harry H. Wimbley. And right at the bottom of the page there was an additional line which went—'Agent for Harry H. Wimbley, Harry. H Wimbley. All enquiries to Harry H. Wimbley'. But you see, it worked, as relentless advertising always does. Even after all this time, I remember him yet.

It is always fascinating to see a real professional at work, no matter what his trade. A few years ago, Devon friends of mine, a couple called Packman, were motoring to Wales and, stopping en route at a pub for a drink and a sandwich, got into conversation with a stranger, 35, trim, neat, smartly dressed, but, in the Edwardian phrase, 'difficult to *place*'. Would they, he wondered, very kindly give him a lift? He was trying to get to Chepstow races. Oh, er, well, all right. He wanted to be there in time for the first race, ('That's when all the money is about'). Oh, of course, a bookie, or a bookie's tout, or whatever.

Off they set. The bookie, looking anxiously at his watch, kept urging Mr. Packman to drive faster, which he reluctantly did. Too fast, in fact, for in a built-up area a police car pursued and stopped them. Everybody got out, the police sergeant took down all particulars in a note-book and booked them for speeding.

Off they went again, the Packmans fuming and the bookie quite silent. At Chepstow race-course they stopped and the bookie got out. Mr. Packman became angry. 'You might at least apologise. It's all your fault that I shall now be fined and have my licence endorsed'. The bookie smiled. 'Oh no you won't, unless that sergeant has a remarkable memory, which I doubt.' From a pocket he produced the sergeant's note-book, flipped it through with a little laugh and tossed it over his shoulder into a deep ditch. He strolled towards the entrance and turned. 'I expect you wonder what I am. I'm a pickpocket. Good-bye, and thanks for the lift.' He passed swiftly through the gates and was lost in the crowd.

A sudden thought came to the Packmans. Mr. Packman felt for his wallet: Mrs. Packman's hand flew to her diamond clip. No, everything was still there. One good turn deserves another.

SAINTS ALIVE

Ever selfless in the service of others, I keep, as you know, a sharp eye on the government expenditure that is lavished on public dinners and the exact extent to which your and my money is being thrust, in comestible form, down other people's throats. It is with some dismay therefore that I note that, not long ago, the Secretary of State for the Environment, whatever that may amount to, 'threw' a luncheon at Admiralty House in honour of a Norwegian environmentalist, a Mrs. Gro Harlem Brundtland. Now why should he do that? 10 other guests. What did they munch and at what cost to us? It took place, it is true, on the Feast of St. Sigismond of Burgundy, but I hardly see why this happy event should be a reason for Dr. Shirley Summerskill and Lord Duncan-Sandys to go along and get a free tuck-in. What further beanos are planned? Will the Feasts of St. Ildefonso of Toledo and St. John of Nepomuck cause hospitable stirrings in the breasts of the Home Office or the Min. of Ag. and Fish ('cod's off')?

If my mind is full of Saints, it is because I have just been pondering on Southampton's splendid Cup Final victory (so jolly when an under-dog wins through), a popular result to which the newspapers did full justice: 'The Saints Go Marching In', etc. And how admirable too were, in defeat, the dignity and warm generosity of Manchester United. How moving it can be when something agreeable happens and everybody behaves well: so much more emotional than supposedly sad and tear-jerking occasions (old grannies can, in the due course of things, die by the dozen and find me dry-eyed). The bearing of the deeply disappointed Mr. Docherty was saintlike. St. Tommy of Manchester? Perhaps not, but only because there are already such a bewildering array and multitude of them.

A painful death is the Number 1 requisite of a really solid saint but some of them have proved tiresomely bounceable and difficult to dispose of. After hitting St. Euphemia sharply on the head for some time with a wooden mallet, they applied a lighted match to her, only to discover that she was entirely incombustible. Hungry lions, starved for a week, were then offered her as their main *plat* but merely licked her feet. Poisonous serpents rather pointedly ignored her, and attempts to saw off selected portions of her were a complete failure. Artists depict her as going in for rather showy clothes, her survival-kit including primrose yellow hostess gowns, flowing white veils and crimson bridge-coatees. They caught her napping in the end (with a sword) but she still wasn't totally done for, her relics, thrown into the sea by Leo The Iconoclast, suddenly popping up again on the island of Lemnos. There's resilience for you!

About some of the saints I am not entirely happy. It is true that St. Bavon of Ghent latterly lived solely on wild herbs and perched permanently in a hollow tree, but he did have a full fifty years of glorious dissipation to look back on and was, I dare say, glad of a breather. Though St. Bernard, finding himself in an excited state after feasting his eyes on a beautiful woman, rushed full tilt into a wintry pool of icy water and stayed there until the feeling, indeed all feeling, had passed, we are not told what steps he took, if any, during outstandingly clement weather. I would have more confidence in an all-the-year-round discourager. And I am unhappy, in a different sense, about poor little St. Reparata (beheaded at the age of 12) to whom the Duomo at Florence was formerly dedicated. Then, as Florence grew in importance, she was brutally downgraded and replaced by a mixed double of a very formidable kind: the Virgin Mary and St. John the Baptist.

Several of the saints have been extremely useful about the house and garden. St. Scholastica, sister of St. Benedict, despite being cluttered up by having a dove at her bosom, was able to cause cloudbursts at will, a real jewel in the crown of any Metropolitan Water Board. St. Alban, too, obligingly performed watery miracles, in a sort of shower of grace-notes, all the way to the scaffold. For marsh draining and general cultivation, apply to St. Guthlac. Worried by foreign squatters? Eviction orders promptly carried out, with ferocious fanaticism, by St. Ferdinand of Castile. St. Swithen, as a second string to his bow, can restore broken eggs, St. Walburga supplies medical unguents of a bituminous nature, St. Hyacinth is a fine travel guide (Denmark a speciality) and, should you find a large and venomous spider in the biscuit barrel, St. Norbert will swallow it down in a trice. Though we are told that St. Francis Borgia encouraged agriculture and founded schools, one would need to know just that little bit more about him before joining him at a mouth-watering cold buffet.

If only, alas, some of the names sounded a pinch more homely and melodious! What, for example, can one make of St. Ethelberga of Barking (a great reader), St. Modwena of Polesworth, St. Swidbert, St. Willibald, St. Polycarp (star billing in the amphitheatre on men-v-animals nights) and St. Phocas, while those who have suffered from French taxi-drivers, both in peril and extortion, will be outraged to hear of the existence of St. Fiacre (Irish, but domiciled in Paris).

Some names instantly strike a chord. What nervous traveller can ever hear the name St. Pancras without glancing anxiously at his watch? And what of little St. Vitus, baptised a Christian at the age of 12 and then thrown by his furious parents into a dungeon (his father, peering through the keyhole, was amazed to see him dancing a wild 'excuse me' with seven angels)? Immersion in a cauldron of boiling oil put a brisk stop to all that capering, or perhaps momentarily increased it, St. Vitus living on as a substitute for the alarm-clock. Heavy sleepers, anxious to be up betimes, can invoke his aid and receive some really deafening early morning farmyard crowing.

One hunts in vain for news of the life and martyrdom of St. Leger, only to find that the race was named, in 1778, after Colonel St. Leger. And though St. Patrick's cabbage (London pride) and St. Agnes's flower (a snowflake) are pleasant enough, not all saintly prefixes have agreeable associations. Do you realise that if, after St. Martin's evil and St. Hubert's disease, you make acquaintance with St. Johnston's riband, you would in fact be drunk, suffering from hydrophobia, and dangling from the end of the hangman's rope?

TAKING LIBERTIES

I really rather like an amusing prank of the kind frequently invented by undergraduates. Cambridge has an enviably high record in this respect. There was the morning when the sun's bright rays illumined a gleaming Austin Seven car, carried up in sections and assembled during the hours of darkness and now splendidly visible for all to admire upon the roof of the Senate House. And there was that moment in the Twenties when the entire undergraduate population gathered towards midday in the market place, summoned thither by word of mouth and assembled nobody knowing quite why. Then, as the city clocks boomed out 12, weird noises rang out from beneath the paving-stones and, to a loud banging of drums and blaring of trumpets, King Tutankhamun and his swarthy entourage were seen making a stately ascent into the light of day up the steps from the underground Gentlemen's Lavatory, itself mysteriously dim and tomb-like. They had not, alas, with them either mummies or treasures richly wrought in gold but they had done the best that ingenuity could devise with items of bedroom furniture.

The whole charade was, of course, in aid of something or other. Whenever, in an Exeter street, I am held up to ransom by bands of students quaintly dressed and charitably collecting for some good cause, I give in a manner which in my little 'group' ranks as generous (20 new p). But not all pranks have generous objects. One of the best of recent years passed almost unnoticed in the newspapers. We all remember the famous photograph of somebody scuttling hastily down the steps of the Tate, picture in hand, but the episode of which I write was the exact converse of this. An art student, wishful for a wider recognition of his talents, strode bravely into the National Gallery with one of his own pictures, found an empty space on a wall, hammered in a nail and promptly hung up his painting. It is said to have remained there for 17 days before anybody, other than art-lovers, noticed it.

Coronations have always been an ideal moment for pranks, with wags dressing up elaborately as eastern potentates and, with no court official daring to question whether they are in truth the Rajah of Rumti-Poo, finding themselves bowed into places of honour and a front line view of the bizarre ritual. At the most recent coronation there was at least one eastern potentate whom nobody could doubt—the wonderfully cheerful, dusky Queen Salote of Tonga, scornful of closed carriages and disdaining umbrella and macintosh, beaming away and wildly waving, a sodden mass of finery with the rain pouring relentlessly down her charming face. In front of her in the carriage sat a diminutive black equerry. 'Who's that with her?' somebody asked Noël Coward. 'That', said Mr. Coward, 'is her lunch.'

I was lucky enough to watch the coronation procession from my club in Pall Mall (how *happy* the Queen looked. It cheered the heart to see her). Drinks flowed, many toasts were drunk, and as the day wore on I became aware that a revered member, Mr. A, having done his dutiful share of loyally toasting Her Majesty, had now decided to take a refreshing nap, his choice of an ideal spot on which to recline being the mat immediately inside the double doors that led to the street. An hour or so went by and I became anxious about him. Ought something to be done? I approached the club secretary and passed on to him my disquiet. 'Is Mr. A breathing?' asked the secretary. 'Oh indeed yes. Actually, he's snoring rather loudly.' 'Is he being a nuisance to anybody?' Well, people coming in and out had to step over him, I explained, but that simple procedure could hardly be described as a nuisance. 'In that case', said the secretary, 'I shall do nothing. If a member wishes to lie down and sleep anywhere in the club, he is perfectly free to do so. Good afternoon to you.' I had been ticked off. It was a fine lesson in personal liberty.

We should all be growing increasingly exercised about preserving our liberties. One can no longer, it seems, sell a possession to whom one wishes. Not a house, anyhow. And, in the matter of houses, what else would one not be allowed to do? Moving about London, one is constantly finding on house walls those agreeable blue and white plaques announcing that this or that prime minister or actor of note lived here (there's a fine crop at the Sloane Street–Pont Street intersection, by that hotel where poor Oscar was arrested). For some time now, I have been urging my pleasant friends, the Hendersons, resident in a trim 'terraced home' in S.W.3, to put up a similar blue and white plaque saying 'Tim and Dorothy Henderson live happily here?' Now, what do you suppose would happen? Whence would come the first cross-patch rat-a-tat on the door instructing them to take it down? For come it would, who can doubt. And why? What conceivable wrong or damage would they be doing? Just a harmless prank.

I have come to loathe and be suspicious of all officialdom. 'They' are there to do us down in one way or another. I had an early example of them at work, in this case the War Office. After a skirmish called Dunkirk, those fortunate enough to emerge were issued with a list of clothing (we were mostly left just with what we stood up in) for which a claim might be made. On the list were '6 handkerchiefs'. I duly claimed for these and other missing items. In a week or so, a peremptory letter arrived. I could only have five handkerchiefs, as 'one handkerchief should have been carried on the person'. There's clear thinking for you.

In the old days, the Foreign Office used to own a de luxe country establishment to which hopeful examinees for the service were sent to discover whether they knew the accepted way of handling knives and forks at dinner. It was rumoured that explosive foods were provided to discover whether they said 'pardon' after hiccoughing. I have a theory that somewhere, in affluent Hampstead perhaps, an expensive residence has been taken over, known as Horrid House, to which all government and county councils are sent for a final course in nastiness (all those even capable of smiling are instantly ejected). How else can one explain the uniform chilliness of the letters they write and the odious attitudes of the writers? 'I am to say that...' 'Doubtless you are familiar with form 784/P/42(b)...' 'We are at a loss to understand...' 'Unless you remit...' and so on. Never a helpful phrase. Not even a cheery P.S. ('Have you recently had rain? Here, alas, we are as dry as a bone!'). Everything rude and hateful. Nasty and getting nastier. Let those impertinent tax officials watch out for trouble when they come bursting into 'Myrtlebank' uninvited and start riffling through my 'things'.

HEAVEN KNOWS

'I don't care what anybody says about God,' announced the late Godfrey Winn in one of those boyish bursts of confidence of his, 'he's always been awfully sweet to *me*.' And it cannot be denied that God really did Godfrey proud, allowing him to acquire considerable fame and fortune from a talent that could, like that daily pinch of Epsom Salts, comfortably sit on a sixpence. But is there a God? At Eastertide the BBC kindly discussed this problem at some length, airing the views of various eminent *penseurs* and they themselves ending up, naturally, on the fence (they'd have been altogether clearer in their minds about it in Reith's day: or else). At one point, diagrams appeared, and pointers, and it was 'therefore this' and 'therefore that', a sort of logical demonstration, and one wouldn't have thought that, against the merest whiff of logic, the idea of a kind or just God stood an earthly chance.

Still, it was sensible of the BBC to discuss the possibilities, and in a tactful manner. They were, on another occasion, less tactful. Easter Day. Glorious sunshine. Everywhere in churches, lips were being moistened and lungs filled for 'Jesus Christ is Risen Today'. The 8 a.m. news. Peep-peep-peep, and then what as Item 1? An Easter greeting? A joyous carillon? An Archbishop (paid to do such things) wishing us well? None of these pleasant subjects. 'The penalties for drunken driving are to be considerably increased.' So much for the Easter spirit.

How, one wonders, is Godfrey, a firm believer, faring? He took, as so many of us have done in our time, the mundane view of heaven—a permanent sunshiny bank holiday and picnics on a cloud with Mozart ('Who's for another sardine?'). Indeed, our only really recent news from the celestial regions comes via the musical Mrs. Rosemary Brown, that lady who takes down scores from assorted 'dead' composers and is the chum of Liszt (so helpful to her in the Balham supermarket). Her psychic information is that everything up there is much the same as down here, only more so. Well, we shall, or shall not, see.

I suppose that, for those of us who do so, abandoning any idea of personal immortality constitutes one of life's milestones. Another memorable moment along the road is the sight of one's first corpse. This far from frightening experience came my way when I was 12. I was at a prep school on the Hampshire coast and every Sunday afternoon we were herded, in an untidy and reluctant crocodile, out for a four mile walk, a master bringing up the rear to encourage stragglers. Our walks were always either Eastward Ho for Gosport or Westward Ho for Southampton. We never, for some reason, went Northward Ho, and Southward Ho would have landed us in the Solent. On this particular occasion there was a pink uncertainty called Mr. Lowley-Jones ('Slowly-Joe' to us) in charge. My friend Williamson and I had been instructed to lead the procession (it was Westward Ho) and, anxious to get back to our tuck-boxes and photographs of Dorothy Dickson, we set a brisk pace, the road hugging the shore.

Rounding a corner, we saw lying on the shingle at the high tide mark, a dead body. The waves had obligingly washed it up and deposited it, in full view, just in time for our walk. Oooh, look! Despite shrieks of 'Boys, boys, come back!' from Mr. Lowley-Jones, we broke ranks and rushed forward, not at all in ghoulish relish but simply out of interest. A woman. Straggly hair. A general puffiness. About 30. Fully clothed. Too bad that we had all written our Sunday letters home. This little happening could have made a striking paragraph sandwiched between the results of football matches. Next week, perhaps.

With some difficulty we were dragged away from this unusual treat but not before one had become aware of the extraordinary *nothingness* of a dead body. It could have been anything, any person, any sex, just a sandy mound of emptiness, occasioning neither alarm nor sadness. And this feeling has remained with me, even when faced with the bodies of those one has loved. Nothing, so to speak, there. A stranger meets one. The spirit has either vanished for ever, or is elsewhere. My second corpse came ten years later. The agreeable Oundle housemaster, to whom I had been appointed house tutor, suddenly upped and died, aged 52. The funeral arrangements necessitated my seeing him. But he wasn't there. A quiet nothingness lay upon the bed.

As a boy at school in the delightful market town of Oundle, the last class of the morning, 12 to 1, was enlivened by the tolling of the 'passing bell'. Midday would boom forth from the very fine parish church clock and then, if a resident had died during the night, the age of the deceased would be rung out for all to hear and marvel at. A far from popular master was known to be 47. As we counted, and the number of years reached the forties, excitement mounted. But alas, never any luck: on the bell went.

Who, one idly wondered as the lesson began, had 'gone'? We knew most residents of course by sight. It was not, we hoped, the cadaverous, spooky gentleman who had a walk reminiscent of that of a kangaroo when about to start some really serious hopping. He was dressed from head to foot in black, said 'Good afternoon' in sepulchral tones to all and sundry and, when not in the Methodist Chapel, haunted the churchyard. There he had once been so enflamed by the charms of a canon's widow bending over a grave to freshen some nasturtiums, that he had attempted to press his suit (black) upon her. Her screams brought aid and her beau was speedily felled to the ground by the art master in full view of a class of boys diligently sketching the west doors of the church. That was a day and a half!

Or could it be somebody known to us as 'Ma Whoop', an engaging gypsy-like, perambulator-pushing lady of advanced years who, to all questions or observations, merely answered with an extremely loud and wild 'Whoooop!', a sound irresistible to schoolboys. Oundle streets rang perpetually with her whoops. Sadly, and in due course, she died (86) and we wondered what she had really been called. Enquiries were made. It was quite an ordinary name but it had been used by somebody else. Gladys Cooper.

SYBIL

A few weeks ago, in a piece called 'Ichabod', I wrote in these pages* of a 1964 theatrical disaster, *Season of Goodwill*, for the failure of which, having written it, I was entirely responsible. I did not on that occasion give the honoured names of the leading players, not wishing to involve them further in the unhappy business but now circumstances make it necessary to reveal them. I was lucky indeed. They were Gwen Ffrangcon-Davies, Paul Rogers and Sybil Thorndike. Sybil's husband, Lewis Casson, came to rehearsals, a helpful presence, and also out on tour with us before we opened in London.

At first I called her, of course, 'Dame Sybil' but that was soon swept aside ('just Sybil, dear: it's *easier*'). I had seen her many times on the stage, sometimes over-acting like a mad thing (as Lady Bucktrout in *Short Story* in 1935, I seem to remember her, though I may be wrong, bending down and looking backwards through her legs at the audience), sometimes marvellously restrained and effective, especially as the bitter Mrs. Whyte in *Waters of the Moon*. I much regretted not having seen her as St. Joan but I was 13 at the time and my theatre-going was dependent on the kindness of parents and jolly aunts and uncles who tended to think in terms of *No No Nanette* and *The Farmer's Wife*.

In her acting there was often an amateur element of enjoyment. Her son, John Casson, has written of a 'hockey-girl heartiness' in her. Amateurs like what they are doing, otherwise why would they bother? True professionals are coldly removed, carefully watching from outside what they are up to. Their only enjoyment comes, if it comes at all, when, after the performance, they feel relaxed and, perhaps, satisfied. Sybil really loved it all the time—before, during and after. It was all a sort of *lark*. Most

* See page 24

of those wild chuckles and, even, cackles, came from the heart and were no part of theatrical art.

She became beautiful as she grew older. In youth it was too strong a face for beauty, but the white hair, the softened outlines, the charming smile produced, with the St. Joan aura which never quite left her, indeed a saint-like look, which bored her. 'I do wish people wouldn't keep calling me a Saint. I'm no such thing. You just ask Lewis!' I did not ask Lewis. As she walked the full length of Westminster Abbey after the memorial service for Sir Lewis, she flashed looks of comfort to those near her as she passed. Upheld by the religious faith she had all her life, she was beautiful indeed. I wrote her, one of hundreds to do so, a letter of sympathy and begged her not to answer. But of course she did.

We had a happy tour with the play. She had friends everywhere, immediately recognised and remembered and many of them in good works ('Oh, hullo dear! Still doing your wonderful work for the blind? That's the stuff!'). Sometimes on stage things went wrong. On the second night at Brighton, Sybil dried up completely and, unable to hear the prompter valiantly prompting, marched over to the prompt corner and had a good look at the script. The audience, happy as audiences always are when anything unusual happens, applauded wildly (stage cats are very apt to make a stately entrance through the fireplace and over an apparently blazing log fire and, settling themselves well downstage, start to clean themselves. This is the making of any play.). Then, one night in Leeds, Gwen tripped over behind the sofa and entirely disappeared from view. Sybil came right out of character (they were playing two ancient American ladies from the northern state of Minnesota), leant over the sofa's back and said, in bracing English tones, 'Are you all right, dear?' Gwen, struggling up and realising that the play must at once be got back somehow into America, answered with 'Ah sure am. Ah didn't hurt mahself none', plunging us, I fancy, into the deep deep South. One always felt that Sybil could not only carry off any stage mishap but would thoroughly enjoy it too ('Didn't they *roar!*').

She had a heart the size of the Albert Hall and her politics, as far as they could be said to exist, were part of the pattern, left of left and practical as well as idealistic. She wanted everybody to have everything. Few actresses (a star for over fifty years) have had longer careers or can have earned more in their time but I much doubt whether anything substantial remains. Money was for giving away. She would have thought it rude and unkind not to answer a begging letter, and they were frequent, without enclosing a little something. Almost anybody with a Cause of any sort got her support. Wild eccentrics, misguided or not, appealed to her crusading spirit (even the egregious Montague Summers was a chum). It was typical of her to take Greek tragedy to Welsh miners and make them enjoy it. In everything of real importance she and Lewis thought as one. They were unworldly. On the day when Sir Lewis was knighted (as he went across the Palace courtyard, Sybil muttered, 'I bet he hasn't got a handkerchief'), he had to be gently discouraged from making a stirring speech for Labour (it was the night of the land-slide victory in 1945) at a celebration dinner in the Savoy Grill, not perhaps the absolutely ideal setting.

I went to see her last October, taking a melon with me ('Lovely, dear. Kind people will keep bringing flowers'). She was propped up and, uncomplainingly, in constant pain. She had had her lunch and had been got ready for the afternoon, when it was hoped that she would doze a little. Her brain and memory were both working splendidly, and her great age had done nothing to change her smile. We talked of Lewis: it was such a relief to her that he had gone first ('He could never have managed, dear'). We talked of her Chelsea life and of the disappearing King's Road shops ('All these *odd* clothes everywhere! They've taken away my dear old grocer and those *darling* vegetable people'). We talked of various parts she had played, in particular Miss Moffat in *The Corn is Green*. We talked of our tour together and I apologised for all the trouble I had given her and Gwen and Paul, and all for nothing. She reached out and patted my hand. 'Nonsense, dear. I enjoyed every moment of it. It was a lovely play. Didn't we have fun!'. She closed her eyes and put her head back. It was the moment for me to tip-toe away. It is not uncharacteristic that the last word that I ever heard her say was the word 'fun'.

BRACE YOURSELF

In the dear old dead days of long ago when British Rail made money, worked on steam and called itself the Great Western, the L.N.E.R. and so on, there were trains that went not only inter-City but to all parts and the attractions of the various parts were colourfully advertised on station platform hoardings. Marcel-waved bathing beauties lured travellers to Bournemouth. The front at Brighton, with a view of the Hotel Metropole, sent business men's pulses racing ('I have to be away for a few nights, my dear'). And 'Come to Skegness' a poster used to say, adding 'It's so bracing'.

And so to bracing Skegness I've finally got, kindly invited to the Butlin's Holiday Camp there by its Public Relations Officer, a genial and intelligent Scotsman and a keen N.S. reader. From my arrival at the Main Gate, where the flags of all nations flap merrily in the bracing breeze, it was smiles and courtesy all the way. The vast establishment, jammed with humanity and all firmly wired in (not to stop them getting out but to discourage gate-crashers), stretches, hugging the sea-front, as far as the eye can see which, in flat Lincolnshire, is very far indeed. At peak periods it can hold 12,000 holiday-makers (a staff of 2,000) and it was easy at first to get lost. Indeed, shown to my chalet (X 25, complete with bathroom), I became briskly disorientated. One row of neat chalets (roses climb up them) is very like another, but I learnt to associate my own row with, at the entrance to it, a chic boutique selling Be Gay Shoes ('Give your feet a holiday too!').

The male and female staff who run the games and generally act as hosts—what the frogs call *animateurs*—are known as Redcoats and one of my anxious fears was that of being set upon by a buxom lady Redcoat who, with a glad shout of 'Cooom on, Grundud' would force me to join other senior citizens in a boisterous Knees Up Mother Brown. I had, in fact, prepared an escape excuse ('It's my silly old leg, I'm afraid. The war, you know. Just one of the many that Jerry's machine-guns didn't miss'). But nothing of the sort happened. No such unsuitabilities occurred and in the chalet lines there was great camaraderie and warmth, with 'hullo hullo' from right and left, introductions and hand-shakes ('Pardon a sticky paw') and offers of reading matter ('Would you care for a squint at my *Mail*?'). One recognised immediately a fine *esprit de camp*. Children everywhere, and very well behaved. Sound-proofing tip-top. From next door, not a transistor, not a cough, or snore, or worse.

Lunchtime, second sitting, and I make hungrily for the York Dining Centre and row 18, table 9. Steaming pots of tea grace every meal, with vinegar and tomato ketchup at the ready, and to anyone with a wide experience of schools, public or otherwise, the food would come as no surprise: good, straightforward, choiceless nourishment guaranteed to tide one over, replete, until the next intake. It is not, perhaps, for the gourmet stomach, but then why should it be? For any birthday or wedding anniversary we rejoice communally. The Redcoats enter in procession, to cheers and clappings, bearing glasses and a festive bottle which certainly looks like champagne but must I think be *un vin mousseux quelconque*. The happy recipients pop the cork, which hits the ceiling. More cheers. At the next table a large and cheerful Birmingham family are making much of a tiny Asian child with huge dark eyes. 'If we hadn't brought him, he wouldn't have got a holiday, you see. We thought he'd miss his mum but he hasn't cried once, not once, have you?' Violent gurglings and another slobbery spoonful of chocolate ice-cream ('Ooops! We nearly had it all down your front, didn't we?').

When dealing with children, the Redcoats are at their splendid best and rate uncle and aunt status. On the greensward outside the dining centre, about thirty little entranced tots are being instructed in ring-a-ring-o'-roses. No pupil power here: friendly discipline prevails, with happy results. Among the afternoon's many attractions is a fancy dress competition for children in the Empress Ballroom. Uncle Leslie officiates, assisted by Auntie Tina, Auntie Jackie and Auntie Dot. Long hair and costumes cause occasional confusion. 'And what's this little girl's name?' 'Greg. And I'm a boy.' 'And this little chap?' 'Joanne. And I'm a girl.' Even the winners, a fig-leaved Adam and Eve are not, at the age of five, too precise. The camp photographer, Uncle

Kevin, clicks ceaselessly and Auntie Dot moves among us deftly selling raffle tickets for a motor-car (proceeds to charity). At any time of day the Redcoats are band-box clean and smart. The lady ones dutifully balance themselves precariously on modish platform shoes but nobody comes a purler.

The evenings bring innumerable pleasures. There is, of course, bingo (in the Regency Bingo Lounge). There is the Gracious Lady (over fifty-five) Contest. In the Bier Keller you can singalong with Baron Wolfgang's Oompah Band, the Baron and his instrumentalists heavily disguised in Tyrolean rig, with much waving of beer *Steins*. There is the search for the camp's jolliest fatty of the week ('The most Cheerful, Charming and Chubby Lady'), the contestants being tickled into hysterics by personable male Redcoats. There is the stately decorum of Old Time dancing in the Regency Ballroom. There are films and stage shows. Additional food and drink are enormously obtainable and a young man wishing to cut a dash with that attractive girl in chalet P 48 can whizz her to the candle lights and sweet music of the Golden Grill. And there is the competition for the Most Glamorous Grandmother (42 compete, and not the faintest sign of self-consciousness in any of them, in this or any other contests), rightly won by a sensational lady, aged 47 with three grandchildren, with jet black hair *en bouffant* and sporting a black chiffon cocktail dress with mother of pearl embroidery at the bodice. Super legs, Silver shoes, Serene face.

It's all very very remarkable. 'Our true intent is all for your delight' it says in large letters over the Sundae Parlour, and though this is the first and the last we see of Shakespeare, it really tells all. Apart from any extra food, drink and bingo, the week's tariff includes everything—heated swimming-pools, chair-lifts, monorails, gigantic amusement parks, tennis, roller-skating, free nappy washing service, etc. etc. If this now reads like an advertisement for Butlin's, then let it be so. Such benefaction deserves advertisement. Now there was a knighthood that really made sense. The charges are quite staggeringly low. A week in May will cost an adult, all in, £22. Children much less. In September it will cost £28. It's more in more popular months, but not all that much more. The same for everybody. No segregations or graduated scales of charges. All, in fact, one class.

FIRE DOWN BELOW

Some years ago in London, when revues still flourished in Shaftesbury Avenue, there was one with an item called Human Stories, a succession of short vignettes from everyday life. At one point there entered a lady of mature years, her face liberally dotted with acne and wearing a shapeless macintosh. She shuffled tipsily forward and spoke: 'All my life I've suffered from these disfiguring spots on my face. I had tried every known remedy, all to no avail, until one day a helpful friend advised me to drink as much whisky as I could. This I've been doing.' (*Loud hiccough.*) 'As you can see, I've still got the spots, but now I don't give a damn.'

It would have been better for her health had she written to Marjorie Proops (impossible to think of the warm-hearted creature as anything but 'Marje') of the *Daily Mirror*, the kindest, wisest and rightly most famous of advice columnists, now revealing in *Dear Marje* (André Deutsch: £2.95) what it has felt like over the last 20 years to cope as best she could with well over a million cries for help, not all of them about sex. Indeed, her readers have expected her to be a cornucopia of information on every imaginable subject. Should one wear long gloves at a cocktail party? What is a good recipe for yoghurt? If a neighbour 'suggests a deodorant' should one cut her dead? Where is the best place to learn belly-dancing? Should a girl get anxious if her boy friend keeps trying on her corsets? 'One day, even, an hysterical woman rang to say she'd found her husband having intercourse with their dog.'

She started her dazzling career in commercial art and was then invited by a perceptive editor to try her hand at journalism ('I rushed back to Stoke Poges and wrote a thousand words'), and now a bright, happy, gig-lamped and successful face gazes contentedly at us from the dust jacket. Her mail has seasonal fluctuations. July and August are quiet times, ditto December.

January and February, when pockets are empty and spirits low, are the peak periods for wives to be abandoned by their husbands. September and October are busy months with the first results of holiday indiscretions beginning to show ('I met this Spanish waiter and he said he loved me'). The tone of the correspondence has, over the years, become less inhibited: 'Questions about orgasms are now as commonplace as complaints about mothers-in-law.' Working closely with the NSPCC, the Samaritans, Alcoholics Anonymous, Citizens' Advice Bureaux, and so on ('I have found the police enormously co-operative in cases of incest'), the job is really no joke. 'It is a fearful responsibility and I am constantly aware of it.'

And it is, of course, sex that causes most trouble, and here we find Marje at her very best. Her goal is a simple one. True happiness for all, no matter what unusual form it takes, and her colours, flying high, are nailed to the mast. If a chap only gets frisky at the sight of a suspender-belt and high-heeled shoes, don't be a spoil-sport: just pop them on and what's the harm in that? Everywhere there is encouragement to get happily on with it, and women who talk of 'submitting', odious verb, to their husbands or who, indifferent, try to discourage marital overtures, meet with her strong disapproval, firmly expressed:

> Your boredom with sex is pathetic and your age is neither reason nor excuse for it. At forty-three, you should be at the top of your sexual form, eagerly looking forward to lovemaking instead of restricting your husband to a once-a-week ration. It's a wonder you haven't issued him with coupons.

With the shy, Marje is all sympathy, advising cosy 'touching' sessions and thoughtfully indicating the best zones to concentrate on. She is down like a ton of bricks on self-pity ('Stop whimpering!'), is ready to bolster up the faint-hearted ('Get wise and get tough'), and she is a bold champion of the virtues of oral sex and of masturbation (You hear a rattling sound? It is the clatter of dry bones as every Victorian-minded clergyman and schoolmaster revolves briskly in his grave). But don't imagine that just anything goes. She is far from sure about the alleged benefits of group sex, usually a male suggestion ('You've got to be watchful with this high-spirited man of yours').

Those of us who lead what I suppose must be regarded as fairly sophisticated metropolitan lives can have little or no idea of the anxious agonies endured by, say, a lonely bank clerk in remotest Northumberland who, at the age of 18, suddenly realised that he hadn't yet started noticing girls and now, aged 43, has gone right on not noticing them. Sexual misfits are right up dear Marje's hospitable street and there is a sharp rap over the knuckles for two parents who cannot face the fact that they have produced a wonky son who has been fortunate enough to find his own particular happiness:

> You want him to see a doctor? Why? He isn't ill. His sexual preferences are his own business. Love is love, and third party interference, however well meaning, cannot be tolerated by lovers.

Nothing, rightly, must interfere with lovers. A daughter who complains that she cannot sleep because of her love-making parents' squeaky bed ('It's getting on my nerves') receives a crisp answer: 'Stuff your ears with cotton wool.' And likewise the grown-up children who are disgusted because their widowed mother has luckily found a lover ('You have a lot of impertinence. It's none of your business'.).

There is only one thing that really shocks her. Cruelty in any shape or form. Otherwise, human oddities, however outlandish, are merely matters to be either encouraged or advised upon (she doesn't mention necrophily but one feels that she could find a place in her understanding heart for even that weird, and difficult to obtain, pastime). 'I take the view that any kind of love, any warm companionship, must be grasped with gratitude.' Quite so. There are, naturally, those who scoff and she has been attacked by a lawyer, sneeringly referred to as the Queen of the Agony Aunties and asked by what right she sets herself up as an oracle. Let us answer for her. Anybody as reasonable, helpful and open-minded has every right. For many years she has been a positive cascade of wholesome good sense and has done great service. Would to God she were in the Government (all private enquiries discreetly and carefully attended to).

TAKE ME TO A LEADER

A recent letter, rightly given pride of place in a national daily, comes from a worried Devon schoolboy of sixteen and bewails a relatively new English malaise. 'My generation—the much maligned teenager—has nowhere to look for a good example.' General corruptibility and laziness are all around, he goes on; there is a trades union movement which 'has made a mockery of democracy' and everything has led the young to 'a natural distrust of adults'. Sad, and it is a malaise which does not only visit schoolboys. Modern adults can comfortably distrust other adults and also be a good bit short on good examples.

One wonders whether young people, understandably disenchanted with the present, can ever drum up any enthusiasm for past heroes and heroines. A pity if they can't, for history must then make very dull reading.

>   For all of we, whoever we be,
>   Come short of the lions of old, you see

Harrow boys used, ungrammatically, to sing. But who then were these lions of old? For an answer we can hardly do better than to turn to Mrs. Andrew Lang's *The Red Book of Heroes*, the word 'red' merely indicating the rich colour of the handsome cover. The book, lavishly illustrated and intended principally for youthful readers, appeared in 1909 and Mrs. Lang's wholesome, pious tone and general attitude to life are made clear in a thoughtful Preface: 'It is common to sneer at "earnest workers", yet where would we be without them, especially in our climate?' This grateful word is intended, we must assume, for miners and coalheavers and snow-shovellers and so on. Her heroes, too, are earnest indeed and 'stainless scutcheons' are the things to aim at.

For starters, Mrs. Lang plays a trump card—Florence Nightingale, illustrated as simpering and lamp-slung, and with nothing in the text to give the tender reader too much of a painful jolt.

Even the appalling conditions at Scutari get watered down: 'The hospital was in a fearfully dirty state. And as for rats!' No smells, you notice. Mrs. Lang reminds us of the, to her, delightful custom of calling children after the names of battles. The Crimea supplied 'Alma', which still exists, and she knew of a pair of twins called 'Inkerman' and 'Balaclava'. Just as well that battles in the recent conflict were not inflicted on babies ('This is my son, Arnhem, and over there is my daughter, Bulge').

So stylistically serene is Mrs. Lang that one regrets that she is no longer here to get her hands, as it were, on current potential political heroines:

> This courageous daughter of a retail provision merchant recked little of the scorn and derision that might be her sad lot on becoming leader of an important parliamentary party. With her musical voice and her demure prettiness, and ever *doing the right as she saw the right*, doors opened everywhere to her, as they always will to the truly meek and gentle. In her inspiring presence, faces lit up and, somehow, suffering and need seemed less acute. And her inside knowledge of retailing provisions proved invaluable when making her skilful plans for 'balancing the budget'.

With the rest of us condemned by Mrs. Lang as 'weary camp followers of the Noble Army of Martyrs', she plunges on with her list of dazzlers. There are spirited drawings of Hannibal, son of Hamilcar Barca (last heard of in 1922 and whom I never expected to meet again in this life), and of some whiskery Gauls sneering rather pointedly at the Carthaginian army. There is General Gordon (born, of all places, on Woolwich Common). There is the splendid Howard, of penal reform. And there is the selfless Father Damien, devoting his life to lepers though a bit of a spoilsport in the Hawaian Islands, 'putting down the manufacture of spirits from the ki-tree', a spoonful of which seems to have been able to do the beneficial work of three large dry martinis, and very nice too. It is to him that we owe the extraordinary list of native nicknames given to a class of boys in the school at Honolulu: Mrs. Tompkins, The Emetic, The Nose, Mrs. Oyster, The Man Who Washes His Dimples, The Tired Lizard and Poor Pussy.

When dealing with men, political or otherwise, Mrs. Lang does not falter and, once again, we regret her departure from the scene:

It is not without significance that this sturdy, open-faced son of a Portsmouth seafarer, now promoted to the highest rank and ready to 'go forth' from Number 10 against the sin and misery of the world, should himself have spent many of his formative years afloat, now here, now there. All the world loves a sailor and 'jolly jack tar' is welcome everywhere, those bell bottoms ensuring fun and companionship a-plenty. But many a night, alone on the poop at eight bells, Jim must have dreamed his dreams of greatness. A second Nelson? Another Hood? Or success in a different field? What should be his line? Bluff manliness with an 'endearing grin'? Just the ticket.

On reflection, I doubt whether any of Mrs. Lang's heroes could today strike a spark with the young, and indeed they do now seem rather a dusty little band. But on the other hand, can some of the present-day fascinators, either sporting or musical, really be regarded as heroes? A different noun is required. What, for instance, about that tuneful gentleman from America (name forgotten) who a few years ago hired a large section of the Isle of Wight and, a bewitching Pied Piper, lured the entire youth of England south? At the time, I was staying in a house which owned, so to speak, two teenagers. Of course they set off too (when I asked them where their suitcases were, they looked at me as though I were demented). They returned next day, bright as buttons, in time for lunch. The concert had been super and they had spent the night in the doorway of a Cowes cafe.

I fell to wondering what would have happened if, in the dear dead days between the wars, I had told my parents excitedly that Jack Buchanan was planning to sing out of doors in a damp field near Ventnor and could I go, please? Horror, consternation and instant refusal, the conversation being rapidly switched, to restore confidence, to the latest pronouncement of Stanley Baldwin. Now *there* was a heroic man! The black boots, the pipe, the square face, the connection with Kipling, the extreme sobriety of his wife and her defiantly unbecoming hats—how could any nation ruled by such a man possibly be on the wrong track? In those days, some of us believed, however misguidedly, in our rulers. We were, remember, living in a land fit for heroes, and how were we to know that those black boots concealed feet of clay?

PRESS ON REGARDLESS

I have never been absolutely sure in my mind of what *belles lettres* consist. Dear old Webster (1932) gives 'polite or elegant literature' and goes on to speak of literary works in which 'imagination and taste are predominant'. I had been wondering for some time whether my weekly pieces could possibly rank as *belles lettres* but, as you see, Webster cruelly puts paid to that idea. I had hoped on my demise to be described as 'the occasional belletrist' and to have the description chiselled in defiantly large letters on my tomb-stone. Incidentally, is it still remembered that Dorothy Parker, hilarious even in death, asked to have the following, in the smallest letters possible, on her head-stone: IF YOU CAN READ THIS IT MEANS THAT YOU ARE STANDING TOO DAMN CLOSE. However, come to think of it, Belle Lettriste sounds all too like a make-up name for some failed music-hall lady who now makes a thin living by reading palms and feeling bumps on a ramshackle south coast pier.

My tomb-stone moment can't be all that far away. I am now what is, I understand, known to 'callers' in Bingo halls as clickety-click (66). Contrary to the general belief, there is a great deal to be said in favour of growing old, gracefully or otherwise as the fancy may take one. Press, therefore, bravely on and come on in, the water's fine. Being young really wasn't all that fun. One seemed to have, for one thing, so little control over the movement of one's limbs. Gangling, one was. Advancing timorously and shyly into the Victorian drawing-room of some elderly relation, it was all too easy to knock over and send flying a table laden with cherished bibelots and then crunch one's way forward, in deep disgrace, over shattered fragments of Swansea *bonbonnières*. My Sunday papers inform me that nowadays children of fourteen discuss with their parents, cosily over family tea perhaps, the ideal moment for them to start having intimate sexual relations with somebody (try to be patient, seems to be the general view, and hang on till 16). In my youth such discussions would have been helpful but totally unthinkable. Blushing and spotty among the Swansea debris, one was assumed in those days to have no such ideas, as 'all that' wasn't supposed to rear its horrid head until one was 20 or so. Well, one would have had news for them.

Some of the benefits of age are unexpected. For those of us who, like rare wines, don't travel well and, en route from one place to another have spent our travelling time in a queasy trance, green-faced and heaving on steamer, train or bus (I have even, on a choppy day, been sick in a rowing-boat on the River Nene. Is this a record?), old age brings joyous relief. *Mal de mer* completely disappears with the years. I did not fully realise this until setting out, a few months ago, by boat for Hamburg. A considerable gale awaited us, lurking like a U-boat, near Heligoland and found my *entrailles* firm as a rock till journey's end. Not a single qualm. It was a pleasant surprise.

Hamburg provided further surprises, not all of them pleasant. Wanting to see what went on at the German equivalent of Madame Tussaud's, I found that I had to cross a busy street called the Gorch Fock Wall, hardly the world's most attractive name. Following the golden rule when abroad of 'cross with the natives', I foolishly put my trust in a small crepe-encased widow who turned out to be a creature of wild abandon, suddenly darting out, me with her, into a dense stream of fast traffic and nearly polishing us both off ('It is being most dangerous coming over, no?' she gasped as we reached the other side. Her widowhood didn't completely amaze me).

Then, to get into the waxworks, I had to push my way past a rather insistent German gentleman who, spying a foreigner, and alone, kept offering me the warm friendship of, apparently, his sister, whom he described as 'appetising'. She was resident, it seemed, nearby and had coffee, cakes and further creature comforts all at the ready.

Within the Tussaud building there was a bewildering array of wax notabilities, all immediately recognisable but, as is the way with these sad dummies, deeply unconvincing. Jackie Onassis could be seen staring hard at Picasso, while Toulouse-Lautrec hobnobbed with Rasputin. Churchill and Lenin eyed one another suspiciously, and, in a dimly-lit alcove, the Kaiser and Hindenburg pored disastrously over their war maps. Gradually

I became aware of a voice from Above (the top floor). Passing Napoleon and Henry VIII, both looking very grumpy, the recorded voice got louder and unpleasantly familiar. Up some stairs, then there they were, the whole grotesque crew—Hitler, Goering, Goebbels, Himmler and Hess, gathered together on the terrace at Berchtesgaden, with Eva Braun hovering demurely on the fringes in an apricot tea-gown. The place was crowded with Germans of all ages and, as the voice rose to a shrill falsetto and was followed by loud Nuremberg cheers, I looked eagerly for reactions, both to the Führer's rantings and the rather bizarre idea itself. Nothing. Faces blank and expressionless. It was almost as though they had no knowledge of who these persons were, no idea who had brought their calamities and the virtual destruction of Hamburg upon them. Odd.

In age one *minds* things so much less. The fire in the blood dies down. Even torch-carrying Mrs. Whitehouse will in due course be glad to stop interfering with what we see, read and hear and be only too happy to return whence she came, settle down in some quiet corner, and enjoy a nice read (I recommend *Rebecca of Sunnybrook Farm*). It's rather agreeable to look back on life's triumphs (nil) and life's failures (847) quite calmly. One of my many failures was the inability to keep accounts of personal expenditures, a practice insisted on at Cambridge by my wise parents and instantly abandoned as soon as I stood, so to speak, on my own feet. I did at one point feel that I ought perhaps to have some sort of idea on what my cash was being so lavishly spent and I bought an account book. I have it still. It contains just the one entry:

Account book. . . . . . 1s.6d.

The only favour one would really like from God, and it's not much to ask, is to know in advance one's own departure date, but this he withholds. But how helpful! Presents here, beanos there ('When are you off?'). No shocks, no surprises. Everything in order. Goodbye goodbye. One could, of course, always take the law, as it were, into one's own hands. But somehow. . .

SOME FINE DAY

The startling and alarming times in which we live do at least achieve something valuable physically: they enure us to shocks. Those with heart conditions now palpitate a good bit less. Though even during the worst of the war, there were, if memory serves, only four daily news broadcasts of importance, nowadays the BBC, a haughty law unto itself, takes it upon itself to hammer out the current disastrous tidings every hour on the hour. The result? Total apathy. Nothing excites, nothing interests us any longer, not even if delightful Angela Rippon, her eyes glittering like nuggets of anthracite, were to inform us that the Titanic had floated to the surface and that all on board were alive and kicking (kicking that daredevil Captain, I should imagine, and demanding their fare money back).

But there was recently just one rather unusual news item which was of particular fascination to lovers of both opera and games. This was that Madam Butterfly's devoted hand-maid, Suzuki (also known, in the flowery Japanese way, as Miss Gentle-Breeze-of-Morning), had apparently changed her sex and was playing in the recent British Open Golf Tournament at Royal Birkdale and doing, what is more, extremely well. And there he was, N. Suzuki, equal 10th in the final result and scooping up £1,975, changeable into yen at what I suspect to be a very adventitious rate. The competitors stayed, I assume, in plushy conditions in nearby Southport, but doubtless loyalty to his mistress Cho-Cho-San, drove Mr. Gentle-Breeze out onto the waterfront just in case B. F. Pinkerton's boat should be putting in, the burly American lieutenant ready at last to do his duty as both widower and father to his son (the little chap must now be nearing the age of 72).

Let us hope that operatic characters do not in future merely confine themselves to golf. With Montreal coming up, what about Brünnhilde for the Decathlon, the all-purpose, multiitemed athletic competition? I have never yet seen a Brünnhilde who didn't look as though she were capable of putting the shot clean out of the ground. Accustomed to leaping from rock to rock, and singing loudly at the same time, the hurdles would seem to her as unexacting as a Sunday afternoon stroll in the Schwarzwald. What a pity that the Decathlon contains no equestrian event, for here she would really come into her own, particularly in stormy conditions, and put even Princess Anne completely in the shade.

But credit where credit is due and though the BBC's tactless news badgering is reprehensible, their coverage of all outdoor activities is masterly. At football one is right in the goal-mouth with Arsenal, and thoroughly in the way too, I dare say. At rugger, one touches down at breakneck speed with Gareth Edwards. When Spitz streaks up the swimming-pool, one is there, splosh splosh, breathlessly beside him. At the Grand National, one falls at Becher's Brook with the best of them. I used to think that the commentators' ability to gabble out, and without the slightest hesitation, the names of the performers was a brilliant achievement, and when it comes to Peter O'Sullevan and those race horses, a minor miracle.

And then a rather vain thought struck me. To you and me, each horse, as with Chinamen, looks pretty much the same, but to a specialist like Mr. O'Sullevan they are totally different, entirely individual and fully recognisable a mile off on a hazy day. But we are all, more or less, specialists in something. Pigeon-racers doubtless know each bird by sight. The only section of either animals or humanity that I, too, would be an expert at would be musical comedy or revue actresses of the 20s and 30s. Suppose that the Derby had been run, not with horses but with these splendid ladies, I too would have been able to dazzle everybody with my expertise. With the paddock parade safely over, we move, in mounting excitement, to the starting tape. 'They're off, and Phyllis Monkman takes an early lead, with Evelyn Laye going well on the outside. Bunched in the centre are Binnie Hale, Edith Day and Jose Collins, with the back marker at the moment Cicely Courtneidge. On the rails, Jessie Matthews is improving and close in behind her I can see Dorothy Dickson, and there, making ground steadily is the favourite, Gertrude Lawrence.' You see, there's really nothing to it.

It is perhaps at Wimbledon that commentators are to be heard at their best with their informative asides, lowered voices, brief and hushed remarks, and sharp intakes of breath as poor Virginia Wade, looking every year more crucified and miserable, lets us down yet again. But the trouble, paradoxically, now at Wimbledon is that the female players play too well. Apart from the engaging little Evonne Cawley, Goolagong that was and the only person to look as if she might actually be enjoying a nice sunny summer afternoon's game of tennis, all is concentration, fire and frenzy. To win, no matter how unattractively, is all. Furious faces glare at each other across the net as the machine-like banging goes on. British players may not win very often but we can be proud, over the years, of having produced two of the game's greatest charmers, Betty Nuthall and Christine Truman, sturdy, wholesome, jolly, smiling girls who played brilliantly and apparently for the fun of the thing and never seemed much to care whether they won or lost. A game is a game is a game.

But is it? The commentators, interviewing some of the winning women players after their exertions, dealt tactfully with the cross and determined little faces as they, like Oliver, demanded more and charm flew out of the window. Did they deserve more? They seemed to think so. What had they to offer? They hinted, modestly enough, that they played very well. Yes indeed, and that, as I say, is part of the trouble. They are all of a piece. Grace and individuality went out with Maria Bueno. Even in looks it is not always easy now to distinguish one from the other. Like Chinamen.

It was not always so. Not even on a dark night could you have muddled up beefy Mrs. Lambert Chambers, seven times champion, with the legendary Mlle Suzanne Lenglen, who looked like, and floated about like, a ballet dancer and could teach every modern player a thing or two about drama, glamour, excitement, tantrums and, into the bargain, the game itself. Appearing on court in a chinchilla coat if the sun was in, playing in daring calf-length skirts and plunging neck-lines ('Very French', ladies sniffed), sustained by sugar-lumps soaked in brandy and glasses of champagne while her formidable frog parents screamed abuse and insults ('*Imbécile!*') at her from the side-lines, sometimes winning forty games in a row, sometimes collapsing in a heap ('*Je n'en peux plus!*'), you never knew what would happen next. Now, although not then a professional, *there* was somebody who really gave value for money.

MODERN LUXILIFE

I'm beginning to feel, selfishly perhaps, that I'm really rather out of things. Not, I hasten to say, because of any unkindness or cold shoulders in our delightful Devon village of Appleton. The only cold shoulders we know here are dished up for Monday lunch and are munched with what's left of the mint sauce. Everything here is all communal joviality. No sherry party given by the Bultitudes but I am there, sipping my share. My Cousin Madge would not dream of 'throwing' one of her well-known and widely appreciated clock golf afternoons without my presence. At whist drives I am the first to seat myself alertly at the green baize. No. It's just that newspaper and magazine advertisements excitingly reveal to me that a full, rich and infinitely varied life is going on all over the place and that I am missing it.

Take, for example, Personalized Sausages, home-made and very warmly recommended by the press: 'tasted marvellous' glows the *Sunday Times*, while the *Financial Times* chimes in, rather enigmatically possibly, with 'have fun'. Fun consists of a simple, hand operated aluminium gadget, herbs, spices, sausage skins and nutritious matter of your own devising to stuff inside them. A few clicks and twirls and hey-presto, a pile of glossy bangers smiles appealingly up at you. I hardly dare now to have any guests to stay. I can just picture them at Sunday breakfast coldly asking themselves why I haven't bothered to personalize my sausages (I thought at first that it meant that one's name had to be stamped on them but a re-reading of the advertisement shows that this doesn't appear to be necessary).

And then, I feel I can hardly face another of those sherry parties because of the wounded looks coming, and rightly, from my host and hostess. In all these years I have never, at Christmastime, given the Bultitudes a Detachable Moustache Guard ('makes dainty china look even daintier. Fits either side of cup'). Colonel Bultitude goes in for whiskers and a detachable guard, clipped to the Crown Derby, would have been the ideal gift for preventing his wispy embellishment from making messy contact with the bedtime Horlicks. But if, contrite, I invite them in to tea, I have no Telephone Dial Lock to stop them deceitfully putting through an expensive call to Singapore while I am out of the room and preparing the Bee-Zee-Bee honey sandwiches and infusing the P.G. Tips.

How very different my world might have been had I, years ago, taken advantage of the many advertised possibilities, hunting through endless newspapers for pleasing novelties. Instantly a life of unbridled luxury unfolds itself. With my Foot Gloves ('a boon to bunion sufferers') and Ankle Grips ('braces weak joints') firmly in position, I move lithely about, now here, now there, in my genuine Indian moccasins, my important midriff areas secure in their new, vital Athletic Support ('it promotes a feeling of buoyancy'). Pausing for a moment to admire my Japanese Miniature Garden ('complete with tiny pagoda'), my Magnetic Window Cleaner (not, as one initially imagined, a dynamic man with a bucket, but a handy contraption and 'the best thing for windows since glass!'), and, on the nest of occasionals, that tempting bottle of Hostetter's Stomach Bitters, I peer through the Gayline Venetian Blinds, awaiting the Musical Doorchimes that will announce the arrival of the computer-dated girl of my dreams ('There's a Miss Rackstraw to see you').

After beaming a warm welcome to her, my dentures gleaming freshly in the sunlight, I suggest a stroll but first, shall it be the Barathea Blazer ('leisure wear for that informal occasion') or the Bush Jacket ('It's safari time!'). Snug in my All-purpose Mini-Bootees, I push open the 'Chatsworth' wrought-iron gates ('Why should a Duke be the only one to live graciously?'), find some soothing music on my Wrist Radio ('a marvel of miniaturised electronics') and, after sweeping the horizon for a few moments with my Commando Binoculars, I draw Miss Rackstraw's attention to the beauty of my lobelias, each and every one drenched in a pungently fragrant anti-pet Shoo! Pussy spray.

Within the house there is much on which Miss Rackstraw can feast her eyes—my Loft Ladder, my continental-style Decorative Shutters ('Vive la différence' it rather puzzlingly claims), my Tie Tidy, my Wet Look Undershorts. In the bathroom, there are the Slip-Proof Bath ('self-adhesive shapes put paid to those slip-ups'), the silent plumbing ('noisy loos easily hushed') and, ready at any time to spring into helpful action, my lightweight plastic Portable Bidette ('you're sitting pretty').

Ah, dreams dreams! Even if I temporarily leave dear Appleton and travel to London, that impersonal city, it seems that I need not be lonely. Magazine advertisements dealing with the lighter sides of life, assure me that I have merely to step into one of the many Multisex Saunas to find companionship a-plenty. Ladies, and in pairs apparently, fully trained in their exacting art, are waiting to give me an Assisted Shower. Just relax and leave everything to them. I am not quite clear whether this means that they kindly assist me into the shower, or assist me out of it, or assist me while I am, which I can manage only too well, either scalding or freezing myself. Time will tell. And if I'm not feeling quite up to the mark and don't want to stir from my hotel, the ladies will be absolute bricks and will pop over at any time and assist me to have a shower right where I am. Could friendliness go further?

I'm now going to mend my ways and turn dreams into reality. To that end I have purchased a periodical called *Exchange and Mart*. Apparently it appears, and how blind one has been, every Thursday and has been doing so since 1868. Even on the cover there are eye-catching attractions—a portable welder, a mower hone for sharpening my mower knives, and an ocean blue, translucent, nylon mesh swimming pool protector, for which I shall have, of course, to build a swimming pool. Within, all is excitement and enticement. The attention is instantly drawn to a Genuine Surplus Flying Suit, just the thing for that Jumbo trip to Jamaica and it will also serve to put the stewards in their places. Then, for picking off marauding pigeons among my sprouts, what about a Wildcat Hunting Crossbow, complete with bolts (Not Suitable For Children), with cheekpiece, thumb grooves and recoil pad, and which, with a range of a quarter of a mile, will enable me to pick off the Bultitudes' pigeons at the same time. And, for good measure, they shall have a Detachable Moustache Guard as well.

HOW'S THAT?

It used to be generally accepted that, as he lay dying in 1936, the last words of that blameless monarch, George V, were 'How's the Empire?' This was either a genuine request for information or, as has been thought, a merry dig at that most British of prime ministers, Baldwin, hovering in the shadows. Some claim, however, that the words were 'Who's at the Empire?', the failing mind recalling salad day evenings at what was originally a rather saucy music-hall in Leicester Square.

Another interpretation of the barely audible sentence was 'How's that, umpire?', which was not only a tribute to our national game but also a despairing call for an early verdict from the Great Umpire in the sky ('Not out!', who can doubt?). There is a fourth possibility, 'Where's that vampire?', but this, emanating from Oxford and in a decade in which that university can hardly be said to have distinguished itself, can be safely discounted. Myself, I plump for 'How's that, umpire?'

If an extra piety and saintliness is to be noted on this page in the next week or so, it is because I have recently been reading what is, on the face of it, a rattlingly good cricketing yarn called *Baxter's Second Innings*, author anonymous. Not Stanley Baxter or Keith Baxter. A good bit before their time. Not even Rupert Baxter, Lord Emsworth's ex-secretary (he left Blandings Castle, you recall, because the entire household started taking pot-shots at the seat of his trousers with an air-gun). No, just Fred Baxter, a teenage public schoolboy turning out for the first time for the XI and going in to bat in an indefensibly lackadaisical manner (*no pads*, if you please!). The spectators are, and rightly, disgusted ('Does that greenhorn know he's playing a *match*?'). The first delivery, a real fizzer, grazes the stumps, Baxter in defence providing a deplorable exhibition of ineffectiveness, arms and legs in all directions. The second ball 'rose on an inequality of the ground' and Baxter, failing to duck, catches it full on the nut, conks out, measures his length, and comes to in the pavy with a loud cry of 'Where am I?', willing voices informing him that he is in the pavy. He is examined by the doctor ('It may smart a bit'), congratulated on a near escape from death ('An inch to the right and you were a goner for sure') and recuperates in the school sanatorium, Matron looking lively with arnica, iodine and beef-tea.

On the afternoon of the next day, Sunday we note, the weather is unusually sultry and Baxter, 'in a dozy sort of state', becomes gradually aware that on a chair at his bedside is The Captain. Not, I hasten to say, *The Captain*, that delightful weekly magazine which appeared concurrently with the *Boy's Own Paper* and contained fascinating articles with arresting titles—'How to Make your own Garden Volcano', 'With Henderson to Nairobi', 'Why Not Challenge a Chum to Halma?', and, for budding zoologists, 'Can Bats Smell?': or was it 'Do Bats Smell?'

The mysterious Captain, a firm talker but physically somewhat ethereal, chats animatedly with Baxter about cricket, the youngster showing an admirable determination to do better in a second innings and enquiring about the identity of the embryo Larwood who had bowled at him: 'he's a regular demon!' Truer than Baxter thinks.

'I shall begin by telling you his name,' said The Captain. 'It is Temptation.'
'Tim who?' said the boy.
'Temptation,' repeated The Captain.
'Oh!' said the boy. 'I hope you're not going to be religious. I thought we were talking about games.'
'So we are,' replied The Captain, cheerily. 'We are talking of the Game of Life.'

Baxter's actual age is not given but as he has won the Junior Sculling Cup (a wet-bob too, you see) *and* has, apparently, mastered shorthand, doubtless a profitable school 'extra', we can safely assume that he is at the post-pubic stage which considerably widens the range and variety of Temptation.

Having established that the game is Life and that Satan is The Bowler, we move on to a more detailed study. Satan's balls come, we learn, in a choice of three, 'Swifts, Slows and Screws,' and all lead disastrously to Sin. Honour is the middle stump and

Screws are the very devil, pardon me, to play: 'a screw goes wide at first and then suddenly rounds upon you and twists in among your wickets before you know where you are'. Everything clear? And don't be put off if Satan is sometimes misleadingly misprinted as Santa.

Practice makes perfect, goes on The Captain. A softy who never attends the gymnasium or uses dumb-bells gets no muscle in his arm. Push against Temptation and you get muscle in your *character*. 'Temptation is simply mental dumb-bells,' continues our friend, adding rather recklessly, 'stop me if I bore you...' You'll need to know the names of your three wickets: Truth. Honour. Purity. Beware of Slows. They may look harmless but by jove they're not. Don't slog at them. Play carefully and the small insidious sins will never reach your wickets. But heavens, what have we overlooked?

'Baxter, you have forgotten something. There are more than wickets.'
'What?' asked Baxter, puzzled.
'*Balls*,' said The Captain.
Baxter was silent.

On reflection, and considering its place in The Captain's reasoned argument, I think we must, for Balls, read Bails. No sort of use having your stumps sturdily upright if your bails are flying all over the shop. And don't imagine that a dislodged bail lying in the popping-crease isn't going to be noticed. All is recorded.

'There are reporters at every match,' said The Captain.
'No, no! It's a private pitch.'
'But I tell you it's all written down—*all*.'
'How so?'
'On the scoring-sheet.'
'What scoring-sheet?'
'*Your* scoring-sheet. Your *character*.'
'Oh!' groaned Baxter.

On no account be discouraged. Get going with those dumb-bells. Block the Swifts. Mind your Bails. Look out for Screws. Pad up. And in due course I hope we shall all meet at the Lord's.

BAD LANGUAGE

When concocting some sour statement, an activity which is, I hasten to say, seldom my practice, on the frailties of human beings in general, you can bet your bottom dollar, or, in this case, *franc*, that it has already been uttered by dreadful old La Rochefoucauld, that unlovely volcano of bitter observation and caustic comment. What a frightful fate to have been his wife and to have had to start each day by receiving an earful of chilly maxims at the breakfast table ('Do get on with your kipper, Henri'). How sadly typical of the French race, flint-hearted and too clever by half, to have produced him and, clearly, to be so defiantly proud of him.

When I first began learning French, it seemed as though the entire French nation earned its living by cutting wood. Every dramatic frog storyette, either for translation into English or for halting reproduction, after two readings aloud, into French of a sort, featured a poor woodcutter living all on his own (*tout seul*) in a cottage (*chaumière*, f.) in a wood (*bois*, m.), busy chopping from dawn till dusk. Elm? Ash? Oak? One never knew, and just as well as the French trees, mostly masculine, were not easy to memorise. Then one day a mysterious stranger asks for food and shelter. The *pauvre bûcheron* reluctantly stops chopping for the time being and is all smiles and hospitality, providing *un repas simple mais appétissant* and offering his bed, prudently vacating it himself and making do on a pile of faggots in the corner. As at that age one was more or less hungry every minute of the day, the idea of the *repas appétissant* set one madly salivating. Of what could it have consisted? Steak and kidney pie? Grilled sole? Bananas and cream? Dripping toast? Perhaps all four, washed down with ginger-beer.

In the morning the grateful guest proffers a purse of gold, instantly refused, to his saintlike host. The narrative then used to burst excitingly into dialogue, translated with difficulty into suitably old tyme English. ' "Nay, my good fellow," quoth the stranger, "hadst thou thought me the King himself, thou couldst not have treated me more fayrely".' Blushing denials from the woodcutter, fidgeting to get on with his chopping. And so to the dénouement. It *is* the King, of course, inexplicably wandering about in mufti with not a crown in sight, and the woodcutter is whisked away to court and a life of ease—doubtful ease one now realises for this fish out of water among the hauteurs and intrigues and smells of Versailles where the only things to chop are heads. The story wound up, naturally, with a rather questionable moral: Always be kind to strangers as you never know who they may be ('Come *in*, Sir Harold!').

And then, bless me, if early steps in German didn't follow the very same story pattern, with this time the hero being invariably a poor charcoal-burner, a profession the usefulness of which was puzzling, for why should one burn good charcoal? And as the story was German, the King, when revealed as such, came in for a good bit more bowing and scraping and sickly sucking-up to than is available from your proud frog.

If only Latin had contained such a heartening anecdote (' "But I *am* Caesar", announced the bronzed warrior') instead of consisting of isolated sentences largely concerning warfare. The teaching that I received, six lessons a week for seven years, in this charmless subject was really, I now see, disgracefully bad. This, I must allow, was partly due to the fact that, at Stirling Court on the Hampshire coast, the Latin master appeared to change every two terms or so, for reasons unconnected with the teaching of Latin. But whoever turned up, he had graduated in ennui and majored in boredom and it was 'apud' here and the idiotic vocative case there (whenever would one need to address a table as 'O table'?), and ablative absolutes galore, and the Belgae (plucky little Belgium, I always assumed) rather pointlessly attacking ditches with arrows. The misery of it all is with me yet and those mainly responsible for our Latin exercise books bore English names. Even now I flinch at inoffensive persons called Hillard and I shun each and every Botting (they must by now both be millionaires). I waste no time deciphering, even if I could, the odious stuff on the pediments of monuments and on entering Broadcasting House and facing the glowing Latin tribute to the spoken word in general and Reith in particular, I close my eyes. And why, may I ask, are such things put into a language neither beautiful in sound nor any longer spoken, and the meaning of which is vouchsafed only to the highly, and probably expensively, educated. This is class distinction of a flagrant kind, and yet they do it still.

Never mind. Apparently it doesn't matter any more what you do or don't learn. If I've understood the new arrangements properly, any little tot capable of holding a pen and tottering to an examination table can now score an O level in any subject. Picture petite and winsome Dawn Westinghouse, keen as mustard on her work, sitting her O Level Geography. Confidently the dainty mite seizes the examination paper handed her by smiling Miss Prendergast and, with a glad cry, spots that the first question is a 'sitter'. 'Where', it queries, 'is Madagascar?' Dawn deftly clutches her biro, readies the quarto, moistens her lips, writes 'Madagascar is in Surbiton', and hey-presto, she has notched up a resounding O Level Geography (Grade Z). Next day she adds on Maths ('$3+4=187$').

Those of us who have had, and rightly, a good many jolts and bumps and failures along Life's Congested Dual-Carriageway can only view with dismay this soft-soaping of the dunderheaded and the idle. And it's not only in examinations but in public life too. As we flounder about in our sad sea of inefficiency and mediocrity, nobody any longer gets reprimanded, struck, ticked off, booted out, kicked, punished or in any way discomforted. And the rot starts at the top.

And it's for the top that I'd start instituting corporal punishment or, at the very least, the stocks. If inflation goes up, then Denis Healey (ever since that marvellous anagram Competition I can only think of him as Enid Eyelash) gets six of the best. Jolly schoolmasters, whacking away, used to say that by making it painful for people to sit down, you soon, ha-ha, made them sit up. Well, desperate straits, desperate measures. I feel sure there's a Latin tag for that, but kindly don't tell me what it is.

I.T.A.L.Y.

As old troopers will recall, and I mean wartime troopers rather than ancient actors seasoned in theatrical mishaps, British censors were at first somewhat baffled by mysterious initials written on the back of letters from the services. A soldier, after copiously licking the flap of the envelope and sticking it down, would complete the job by adding the letters B.O.L.T.O.P. It was a loving message to his wife and it stood for 'Better on lips than on paper'. Or, with the same theme and procedure in mind, there was S.W.A.L.K. ('Sealed with a loving kiss'). And then there came a new one which, displayed on countless envelopes, considerably agitated the more spy-conscious censors. It was the letters I.T.A.L.Y. What could it be but some devilish message to or from the Axis powers and perhaps old Musso in person? Anxious enquiries restored confidence and revealed a hidden meaning every bit as harmless as the others. I.T.A.L.Y. stood for 'I trust and love you'.

Well, as to the *vrai* Italy, one couldn't, after 1940 and all that, exactly trust it any more but one would be a cold-hearted holiday-maker not to love the place. Here on the majestic Amalfitana coast, just round the corner from Naples and looking onto the bay of Salerno, everything breathes a welcome. The sun shines and the Italian bees, more obese than ours, buzz busily in the bougainvillaea. The plumbago is a riot of blue and wherever it is possible for climbing geraniums to climb, they obligingly climb. We lie out on flat expanses of rock and leap from them into twenty feet of warm and limpid Mediterranean. This morning the hotel lift that descends us to this bathing haven momentarily stuck and those who had read Arthur Haley's *Hotel* wore thoughtful expressions (a lift burst open, you remember, and several hotel guests reached ground level and the reception area rather more quickly than they had planned). But, after various Italian screams and wails, all was to mechanical rights again (unexpected of them, somehow, to be so skilful with machines).

News spreads slowly to outlying rural and relatively self-sufficient districts. At Appleton in dear Devon, the news a year or so ago that the country's dustmen were on strike never got through to our splendid fellows at all and our bins were tirelessly emptied. Here in our Italian backwater, communist gains and upheavals of a political kind in the capital in no way disturb the even tenor of our days and ways. Hearts are as high as the price of drinks. For foreigners, the main excitement for the more fidgety Phils is sight-seeing and coachloads of visitors go east to Paestum or rumble west to Positano along a high and terrifyingly winding coast road where the only sensible thing to do with your eyes is to close them. Zones of Silence display notices forbidding vehicles to hoot at night, helpfully translated for English motorists as 'No Horning after 11 p.m.'.

Every now and then a steamer chugs past, jammed with trippers bound, ill-advisedly in my view, for Capri, that overrated haunt of the would-be raffish, with rather too generous a sprinkling of sprightly, unattached gentlemen and where, unless you do so under the warm wing of Gracie Fields, it is almost impossible to find anywhere an accessible section of sea in which to bathe. The zig-zag walk down from the town to Miss Fields was the grateful gift many years ago of wonky old Krupp, who used the island for activities which satisfactorily proved that you *can* get a man with a gun.

Yesterday our elderly barman, quivering with excitement, announced that today, two miles along the coast, there would be fireworks, and indeed, from dawn onwards, loud bangs have been heard echoing round the ragged rocks. When it comes to letting off fireworks, the Italians, impulsive enough as it is, know no restraint. It is evidently the noise that pleases them most for in the dim light of another day they can hold themselves in no longer and they rush out and ignite several Roman candles and a catherine wheel. During our pre-lunch Campari-soda, an ear-splitting series of explosions and sundry bright flashes can only mean that the set-piece (the Pope, perhaps, chair-borne and in full canonicals) has been prematurely popped off, accidentally on purpose, don't you know. Not even the holy hour of siesta time halts the din and by dusk there can be few fireworks left, and just as well as a sensational thunderstorm sends all but the most dedicated pyromaniacs flying indoors. But even then a few rockets and star-shells go bravely zooming up into the downpour. Our barman, even though busily occupied in hauling tables and chairs in from the terrace and out of the rain, wears an expression of quiet contentment.

It was here of all places that Ibsen, in the Hotel Luna ('Hotel at the Moon' its post-cards say) wrote *A Doll's House*, miraculously bringing with him sufficient Scandinavian gloom to off-set the happy joys of this enchanted coast. There are no longer many Scandinavians about. We have Americans, gig-lamps gleaming and, parents all, apparently quite unaware of the atrocious public behaviour of almost any American child. We have a number of lumpy English ladies with the look of retired schoolmistresses who, there being little terrain that is flat, lumber down and up hills ('I'm going to take this slowly, Edith'). There are a few Germans and a Belgian or two. The hotel menu is a strange mixture of Italian, French and attempts at English ('Veal sweet-bitter', 'Spaghetti tip-tap' and 'House tart' it encourages). And it is a mixture in other ways for we munch cold meats ('English plate') with tunny sauce and boiled hake with mint sauce, both surprisingly toothsome. In the town, those bent on festive gaiety are directed to it by a large and elaborately painted sign saying THIS WAY TO THE NIHGT LIFE which in due course leads dare-devils to a club called LE HOT SPOT. Incidentally, back-street smells are now as nothing to the noisome asphyxiations of forty years ago.

On the town rocks sits a female figure of advanced years dressed in deepest black. Like some enigmatic character in a Maugham short story, she stares, her hands clasped, unwaveringly out to sea. The widow of a naval captain sunk in the Salerno landings? An Italian woman who recklessly gave herself long ago to a German officer who abandoned her? A poetess meditating a sonnet sequence? Better not to know. It's probably just the attendant from the ladies' lavatory taking a breather during one of her rare slack periods.

DOUBLE DUTCH

Now is the time of year when holiday travellers, happily bound for the foreign delights of the Continent, are busily brushing up their French, swotting up their Spanish, and feverishly mastering the German for 'I have quite sufficient sausage, thank you,' or, for those intending to launch themselves into the briny from treacherous Atlantic beaches, the Portuguese for 'My name is Mrs. Henderson and I am staying at the Hotel Splendide. Might I trouble you to summon a life-guard? I am drowning.'

Basically of course every Britisher is still rosily confident that the English language is universally popular and, spoken loudly and distinctly and with much elaborate mouthing as though to a deaf and dotty nonagenarian, will be promptly understood and everywhere acted on.

They feel sure that, for example, itinerant sellers of unusual postcards in the Place de la Concorde will respond immediately to idiomatic discouragements such as 'Buzz off! I have had quite enough of your sauce. Kindly make yourself scarce.'

Sometimes one can get by with an interesting mixture of French and English. I was once on a French cross-Channel boat on my way to Boulogne. Fragrance is not perhaps quite the first thing that one thinks of in connection with any French sanitary system and on this occasion, life afloat was outstandingly whiffy.

I saw an outraged Englishman emerge hurriedly, purple in the face and with handkerchief pressed to nose, from the gentlemen's retiring place, make for a braided and whiskery naval official and furiously speak. '*Sur ce bateau your lavatoires sont absolutement disgusting.*'

He got no change at all. A polite bow and a smile. What, the smile seemed to say, do smells matter when we, the French nation, possess the world's most beautiful language (and they do, too), and which contains the world's most beautiful-sounding word? The word is *'libellule'*. It means 'dragon-fly' and you'll need to have rather a good accent to get the full benefit from it.

The French, unaccountable in so many ways, are a complete enigma when it comes to their reactions to the English people and the English language. By far the most popular post-war foreign minister has been George Brown (*'ce cher et étrange petit homme!'*). They found him quite fascinating and so deliciously surprising and unpredictable (my informant was Nancy Mitford, who lived at Versailles and was much in Paris) and one's astonishment means no disparagement of so jolly a chap. It is just that the brief love affair, which is what it was, seems so improbable.

Then what about the English words that the frogs have decided to borrow from us? In this respect, the French taste and sense of fitness, usually so impeccable, have totally collapsed. Shop-keepers, prudently keeping assorted merchandise in stock, make use of the hideous verb *stocker*. If the shop is a toy shop and caters especially for young children, you can waltz in and say "*Stockez-vous Kiddycraft?*' and not an eyebrow will be raised.

And mysterious indeed is the French relish, increasing with the years, for our word 'standing' indicating a position or grade in a profession or the social world ('What is his standing?'). This is now, on hoardings, a prestige word, with advertisements for *un appartement grand standing* or *un studio* (bed-sitter) *grand standing*; the imagination boggles at what a cramped *studio petit standing* can be like. I have even seen homely pounds of butter ennobled into *beurre grand standing*.

Years ago, when I struggled to teach French and German in an agreeable public school called Oundle, we didn't really care for, in any sense, impure words. No vocabulary that didn't feature in the dignified pages of Racine or Goethe was totally OK with us and where in Racine would you ever find the word '*un dead-beat*'?

And it is indeed in the field of sport that the French quite lose their heads. A football striker, nearing the goalmouth, is encouraged with screams of *Shootez!* Boxing fans clustered round the ring, wait keenly for *le knock-out*, the newspapers subsequently reporting that 'X *knockouta* Y'. Tired after that game of tennis? Heart thumping a bit? Then hurry off to your doctor for *un check-up* and exchange the exhaustions of tennis for the calmer joys of hiking, which comes out in French as *le footing*.

I've never bothered very much about Italian, for what can one hope for from a language where the words for 'very tired, are, if I've got it right, *molto stanco*, words which clearly ought to mean that quite recently there has been present a very nasty smell. Nor do I care very much for a lingo where the word for a splendid handlebar moustache is diminished into the futile little *baffi*, where 'shampoo' comes out as *lavatura della testa*, which might be almost anything, and where 'aft' on a ship is *poppa*.

However, I'm shortly off to Amalfi and I'm taking with me an oldish Italian phrase book which, like most of such things, tends to concentrate on disasters.

From quite small and humble beginnings ('My ballcock is faulty and the bathroom is flooding') we move on to bigger ('My husband has measles') and better ('His temperature is 105') things, conjuring up exciting possibilities in the way of telegrams home ('Come at once, Herbert sinking'). If 'sinking' after passing through the Italian telegraph network, has changed itself by the time it reaches Melton Mowbray into 'stinking', well, that's just hard luck.

I've got a hankering to go, before I die, to Amsterdam and at first sight Dutch seems to be, as a language, all that is most helpful and simple. Take, as an example, an ordinary noun, 'the ghost' which is, in Dutch, *het spook*. *Het* is, after all, merely an anagram of 'the', and *spook* explains itself. When everything is going well we say *Dat is goed*, and look, we're speaking whole sentences right off.

All is plain sailing: Pen is *pen*, bed is *bed*, pan is *pan*, pot is *pot*, sap is *sap* and cat is *kat*. *Het telegram, het gas* and *het menu* speak for themselves. And then, lulled into a feeling of security, the Dutch spring very unpleasant surprises on you. *Het* totally disappears and becomes *de*. Recovering swiftly from this shock, off we go again with *de mist* (mist), *de klok* (clock), *de lamp* (lamp), *de chauffeur* (chauffeur) and then suddenly the carpet (*het karpet*) is pulled from under you.

Bumping by mistake into a stranger in, say, Paris or Naples, a simple *Pardon* or *Scusi* is all that politeness requires. But not in Amsterdam. Here you have to gasp out, if you can pronounce it, *Het spijt me*, which, apart from anything else, sounds in no way apologetic.

All at once the delightfully easy vocabulary (*het glas*: glass) drops right away and the Dutch, our hereditary enemies after all, show themselves in their true colours. What, do you imagine, *de knikker* means? Not what one might happily suppose, or possibly seek to purchase in a shop, but, of all things, 'marble'. Words lose all sense of beauty or decency and become unusual or, as they have it, *onge'woon* (I'll say!). The word for beautiful itself, *mooi*, is highly displeasing. 'The eye' is *het oog*, so presumably 'the beautiful eye' is *het mooi oòg*. I ask you!

There's no end to the nastinesses. What about *het boom* for 'the tree', *het loon* for 'wages', and *de fooi* (the tip)? Possessives are really most alarming, 'Mary's doll' becoming *Marie d'r pop*! The simplest things become a burden: 'because' is *omdat* and 'which' is *welk*.

And, speaking of fish, when you have nerved yourself to dart into the market for a pound of tasty haddock, you find yourself having to stammer out the word *de schelvis* which ought by rights to mean 'shellfish' and nothing haddocky about it at all.

But I must confess that, for some years, merry friends have been preparing me for Dutch oddities. They have assured me that (and if they're wrong, don't blame me) the Dutch for Please Keep Off The Grass is *Nit Brillen in de Bushen* and that 'Mount your horses' in the Dutch cavalry is *Scramble op de beeste*.

We know for a certainty that when the ballet, *Miracle in the Gorbals*, was performed in Rotterdam, it was billed as *Het Wunder in de Schloppen*, and a gifted writer friend of mine whose poems were translated into Dutch with some success, tells me that his delicate lyrics, light as gossamer, tender outpourings of the human heart, appeared under the delightful general title of *Het Tweedy Bundle*.

CURTAIN UP

Loyal readers of this column will, in their tolerant way, have grown accustomed to receiving up-to-the-minute information about my section of Devon rural life with its varied warp and woof. That church fête which netted £108 for repairs to the roof. The arrival of weekly bingo in the village hall ('Tch, tch!' from some). The day when one of Mr. Brickman's vast cows, reaching eagerly for who knows what tit-bit, overbalanced and fell through the hedge into my orchard. And so on. The Bultitudes, incidentally, went to Ibiza ('Where be that?') for their summer hols and are the talk of the village.

And now this loyalty is to be repaid by tidings of an altogether wider and more interesting kind and from beyond, of all things, the Iron Curtain. Permission has been sought by a kind Mr. Dubrovsky to reprint in a Russian magazine a piece I wrote for these pages called *Royal Mail*, which fancifully featured a mother's request to the Queen for her daughter to be allowed to use the Buckingham Palace hard tennis-court. The request was courteously refused. The magazine is called *Foreign Literature* and Mr. Dubrovsky writes from Pushkin Square, which must be in the very heart of Moscow (no postal code, I note). Without so much as mentioning the vulgar subject of roubles, I shall gladly give permission, only hoping that the magazine's readers will realise, which I rather doubt, that the whole thing was intended as a jolly jokeski.

My acquaintance with Russians has been both rich and rare. As an undergraduate, I was assistant stage-manager for an amateur Cambridge production of *The Soldier's Tale*, amateur but for one very notable exception. The wife of Maynard Keynes of King's, recently retired from the Russian Ballet, was persuaded to re-emerge and dance again. Her name was Lydia Lopokova and she had been the Czar's favourite ballerina. She was supremely brilliant and workmanlike and entirely enchanting. She rehearsed uncomplainingly for hours on end. It was surprising to find how nervous she was. We were in a small theatre that seated about 250 people but her stage-fright was Bolshoi-size. Waiting in the wings, she would suddenly flutter away, disappear and return, smoothing her *tutu*. 'I had to pass a little nervous water' she explained ('Very Russian' we said to each other in our prim undergraduate manner).

My second Russian acquaintance was also a dancer. This was pre-war in the South of France when friends of friends brought along one day Serge Lifar, holidaying nearby. He, in his turn, had been Diaghilev's favourite. After dinner it was hinted to him that if he cared to hop a little, it would be highly acceptable. He would and did (it is always the best performers who make the least fuss about unsuitable conditions). We had an excellent pianist and Lifar danced *L'après-midi d'un faune*. We also had the grapes necessary for the dance, real ones and rather over-ripe, which plopped singly to the carpet and made a mess. We also, alas, had a rather foolish woman with us. Lifar said he would dance again, but after a short rest. He was not tired, he said, but had to get out of one mood into another. 'Oh, I see,' she said, in dreadful, rattling English tones, 'you haven't got your second wind yet.' Lifar didn't understand and so she burst into French, mouthing elaboratedly as though to a deaf nonagenarian: '*Vous n'avez pas obtenu votre deuxième vent.*' He was polite enough to smile.

My only other Russian acquaintance was of a very different kind and I met him on a vast and expensive sea-going yacht in Flensburg harbour in May, 1945. The war had been over a mere five days and parties of British and Russian officers had been despatched to the surrendered German high command to request information on this and that (as a German speaker, I had to try to discover where Himmler was, but they knew as little of him as we did). We were billeted on the yacht, which had been Hitler's, and various German generals were summoned in turn for interrogation. Going ashore, it was a weird experience to meet beefy Field Marshal Jodl, still clutching his baton of office, striding alone along the quay towards the yacht. Courtesies were exchanged. I saluted. He touched his cap with the baton. The same with Keitel. They appeared quite unshaken by what had happened and one could but admire their bearing.

We had our meals communally in the yacht's large saloon.

Down one end of it a dozen or so German submarine officers were attending a course on torpedoes. Being German, the course continued because nobody had yet told it to stop. Half way up the saloon stood a bust of Hitler. I found myself munching next to a Russian officer, name unknown but I thought of him as Boris. I attempted conversation. 'What heavenly weather!' No answer. '*Quel beau temps!*' Nothing. The German language was an equal frost. For breakfast one morning, porridge appeared. Boris stared at it nonplussed, as well he might be, and then, seizing a knife, he smeared it on a hunk of bread and got it down. 'Well done', I said, but I might as well have addressed the ceiling.

And then, a day or two later, something rather bizarre happened. We were having lunch ('Another scorcher!' I had tried, but Boris wasn't having any) when two German workmen entered bearing a very large saw. They advanced to the bust of Hitler and started sawing off the head. One hardly knew where to look. The German submariners gazed at their plates. All conversation stopped while we ate silently on. The sawing took some time but eventually Hitler's head crashed to the deck with a loud bang. The workmen briskly gathered it up and exited. Our embarrassed silence was broken by Boris. His shrieks of happy laughter rang loudly out. He found it the merriest treat in years. He banged me on the back, jabbering away like mad. He grasped my hand and shook it. He thumped the table. He brought out vodka and we drank a toast. From then on we were friends.

But that, sadly, is all, though my TV licence renewal form reminds me, oddly enough, of Russia. This strange three-sectioned document bears an almost hysterical plea: DO NOT BEND COUNTERFOIL, and whatever would happen if one did? It lists endless things that I must not do, with or without my TV. It tells me how to pay and where. It bears at the bottom a figure composed, and I do not exaggerate, of 38 numbers and about three inches long. But, exhausted by all this activity, it gives up when it comes to my name. All it can gasp out is the word 'Marsha', and it's 'Marsha' here and 'Marsha' there. Wasn't this, more or less, the name of that doleful character in *The Seagull* who slopped about all day in black announcing that she was in mourning for her life? Thanks very much.

KNOCK KNOCK

Though not by any means a devout believer, I do quite frequently pray. To what or to whom I pray I am far from sure but the results are invariably the same and quite totally disastrous. Take my most recent batch of requests, every one of them turned firmly down. Throughout July I prayed for rain. Sickened by England's humiliations, I prayed that we might win the fourth Test Match. I prayed that one of my few remaining molars wasn't as rickety as it felt (my kind Mr. Bellamy, on examining it, gave a gasp of horror and tugged it instantly out). And I put in a plea for poor old Mars and for there being evidence of somebody or something somewhere that might reduce the world's chilly isolation.

I haven't much faith in there being anything 'out there', so to speak, but I am glad to report that our Devon station-master now has at least a suspicion. Two agreeable American women-friends had been staying with me and, on arrival at the station for their return to London, the ladies could find neither their tickets nor their seat reservations, both obtained from a travel agency. In our distress, we were courteously wafted to the station-master's office, where all was kindness and efficiency and personal attention and where, after a telephone call to the agency, duplicates were provided. By way of explaining their carelessness and their American accents, the elder of my friends leant confidentially towards the station-master, lowered her voice and said 'We're from the other side, you know.' He looked extremely startled, having obviously understood the words as 'the Other Side'. My friends, both comfortably chunky ladies and wearing good serviceable macintoshes, didn't look like what the world considers to be ghosts, but you never know. By this time, the younger one had been stung on the cheek by an angry wasp and, swiftly swelling up, resembled a lop-sided red balloon. Did wasps sting ghosts? Who could say? Who could pronounce with certainty on anything in the spirit world?

Well, quite a lot of people have thought that they could. The entire field of psychical research is now opened to us by Alfred Douglas (nothing at all to do with Oscar's noble chum) who, remaining scrupulously objective, examines in *Extra-Sensory Powers* (Gollancz: £6.95) every facet. Before we get down to the actual table-rapping, we find that history is dotted with rum and inexplicable occurrences. St. Francis could, as we know, take off and hover in the air, beech-tree high. Hot on his heels came St. Joseph of Copertino who, gracefully soaring, notched up over 100 flights. Then there was boastful Swedenborg who cheekily announced a personal visit from the Lord himself. Mysterious and mesmeric Dr. Mesmer, dressed from head to foot in a rather trying shade of violet, used to prod patients with an iron rod and produce contagious convulsions, with the entire consulting-room excitingly a-twitch. Nobody seems to have bothered much about spiritualism until 1840 when an American went into what must have seemed rather a prolonged trance and dictated a massive 800-page work entitled *The Principles of Nature*, and from then on, trances were all the rage.

By 1853 there were 40,000 Spiritualists in New York alone and the din of the table-rapping and ringing of hand-bells, both popular spirit pastimes, must have been deafening. In London the Brownings attended a séance in Ealing and a ghostly hand, after shooting up through the table-top and placing a garland of flowers on Elizabeth's head, had then drifted out of the window and into Hopcroft Avenue. Elizabeth, much impressed, flashed the news by letter to Wimpole Street. Robert, on the other hand, went home and wrote his derogatory poem, *Mr. Sludge, the Medium*. Can it be that women are in general more gullible or, to put it more politely, more impressionable, accessible and sensitive?

It would certainly seem so. Most mediums have been female, and in a serious article such as this we must all strive to forget Miss Hermione Gingold, in crumpled brown velvet and beads, in that Gate revue:

I'm only a medium medium,
I do it to relieve my tedium.

There was Florence Cook (subsequently caught cheating) who insisted, and understandably, on subdued lighting, whose *tour de force* was a curtained alcove at which Eastern heads, all whiskers and turbans, appeared, and who tended to get friendly with male séance-attenders ('Do you squeeze?'). There was Kate Wingfield, a pioneer crystal-gazer, whose specialities were lengthy messages, tirelessly rapped out, from the dead, and the diagnosis of illnesses ('Do watch that chest of yours!') among her sitters. This, at least, was a useful accomplishment for so often mediums' achievements were merely idiotic and nobody's more so than those of Eusapia Palladiso, who shunted about the continent creating havoc wherever she went. No sooner had her séances started than chairs and tables danced about and broke, curtains billowed out, guitars twanged, noises like pistol-shots rang out, invisible hands pinched the sitters, and every cup and saucer in the room shattered into smithereens. Nerves were hardly calmed by Eusapia's ceaseless banging of her tambourine and her loud cackles of maniacal laughter. Alas, she too was caught cheating, supplying loud rapping noises by kicking the table-leg with her sturdy Italian boots, and when outraged sitters attempted to hold her down she 'acted in an overtly erotic manner': and all this in Cambridge too, with the famous magician J. N. Maskelyne present, Eusapia having first, to allay unworthy suspicions of trickery, paraded about in her stays and a short flannel petticoat.

Despite such disappointments and let-downs, the novelty caught on, and in some very surprising quarters. A distinguished lecturer in classics at Newnham received messages through 'automatic writing' (messages in Greek and Latin, natch). E. W. Benson, later Archbishop of Canterbury, founded a Ghost Society. Ouija boards shot about all over the place supplying singularly literary words of comfort ('Rest, weary heart!'). A. J. Balfour, a future Prime Minister, took a lively interest in the quaint goings-on. The frogs got going with planchette. Radclyffe Hall and her side-kick, Una, Lady Troubridge, muscled in. And, most fervent of all, there was Sir Oliver Lodge who, though dead, obligingly popped back again in 1969 with a medium called Mrs. Osborne Leonard, and not a stone's throw from Peter Jones.

Thrilling stop-press news. My prayer about Mars seems to be about to be answered, if in a rather minor way. It appears that there may be an organism there which, if fed with the right stuff, may then give out a sound resembling the tiniest of burps. If it then says 'Pardon!', we're really on to something.

PLEASED TO MEET YOU

Somerset Maugham (a very much kinder man, incidentally, than several of those who have seen fit to write about him have chosen to indicate) used to express surprise at the ordinary person's keenness to make the acquaintance of those who, in this weird world, rank as eminent and famous. I suspect that he was only surprised because he had already met most of them himself, had been amused by their egocentricity, their imperfections and, possibly, their dullness, and was amazed that anybody could wish to seek them out. But a desire in the humble to hobnob with notabilities seems to me to be perfectly natural, however brief and sketchy the hobnobbing may be.

Five years ago I spent a delightful month staying with kind American theatrical friends on the fringe of a small village in a remote part of Wisconsin. It was the highest of high summers, with temperatures in the 90s and I spent much of my time in and around the pool, surrounded by chipmunks, those charming North American squirrels who, in their appearance and quick movements, remind one so vividly of the late Nellie Wallace. The chipmunks were wary of me as long as I was dressed but, stripped for the pool and splashing about in it, they accepted me at once and made friendly overtures. They obviously thought that I was a species of outsize, pink hippopotamus. Part of my agreeable daily routine was to visit the village. The movies had prepared me for it. It was like every one-horse town you've ever seen. There was a sleepy saloon with swing doors, a bank (open Tuesdays and Thursdays), a general store, a tiny hotel, a church, an old-timer snoozing in a rocking-chair, a few houses and that's about all. The only things missing were galloping hooves, bullets and Gary Cooper.

Everywhere there was extreme friendliness. Small children said 'Hi!' and giggled at my answering 'good afternoon'. The man in the bank said 'Howdy!' and, in return, received 'good morning' from me. In the general store (a staff of three) I made a big success. They found my English accent continually fascinating. Whenever I appeared, the staff and customers crowded round me to hear and marvel at it, and an aged grandmother was summoned from upstairs to join in the excitement. As time went on, they plied me with questions. Did I know Tom Jones? I hesitated for a moment between the book, the operette and the film, and then I realised that they meant the pop singer, a great star on American television. 'No, alas,' I said. Did I know Lulu, another telly hit? 'I'm afraid not,' I said. Worried looks. But surely I must know the Queen? I couldn't bear to disappoint them further. 'Yes,' I said, 'but only to wave to.' 'And does she wave back?' 'Oh yes indeed,' I said. This, with them, clearly ranked as hobnobbing and formed an entirely satisfactory and cosy relationship. I do not know what picture they had in their minds. Perhaps they saw me bowling up the Mall and waving from an open car, with the Queen rattling up a Palace window, leaning out with a merry 'Yoo-hoo!', and waving, waving, until I was out of sight.

I find it quite an agreeable pastime, when feeling momentarily lonely or neglected, to hasten to my small cyclopaedia (just the one volume) and let the imagination fly in a riot of hobnobbing with famous human beings of a kind well outside my range. The cyclopaedia contains a section called Prominent People, gathered together by who knows what inventive brain, and listing the widest possible range of interesting historical availabilities: one's social life blossoms immediately. How about a Woman of the Year luncheon with Grace Darling, Cleopatra, Peg Woffington, Florence Nightingale and Boadicea? Guest of Honour, Lady Macbeth (how delightful to find that her Christian name was Gruoch, 'Grouch' for fun, and that they enjoyed 17 years of ill-gotten sovereignty). The list's compiler is, by the way, handy with brisk thumbnail sketches—Louis XV ('most licentious'). Louis XVI ('apathetic and unfortunate')—and, goodness me, the people one has been *missing* all these years: Lord Armstrong, whose new-fangled gun mowed them down so splendidly in the Crimea: Lablache, who taught Queen Victoria how to sing; Cerdic the Saxon who, a striking figure in woad, conquered the Isle of Wight in 530.

For a really grand male dinner party, you've got to be extra careful with your *placements* (a word, did you know, that no

Frenchman ever uses). You shouldn't put Attila (who must, at all costs, be kept off red meat) next to the Venerable Bede, who will be peckish after his strictly monastic fare. Why not sandwich between them Sir Raymond Unwin, who dreamt up those attractive Garden Suburbs? Alcibiades, Socrates's chum, would fit in anywhere and could keep an eye on Rasputin, who can't be trusted with anything on two, or four, legs. At the head of the table? Tutankhamun, of course. And at the bottom, well below the salt, poor old Watts-Dunton, an odd choice and whose only real claim to fame was to keep Swinburne off the bottle. For a floor-show, what about Blondin walking precariously overhead to a musical accompaniment ('Come, Tannhäuser, give us one of your minne-songs!')?

As new editions of the cyclopaedia appear, names come and go from the list. People considered prominent one minute are woefully unprominent the next and right out on their ear. Recently vanished are the Very Rev. Cyril Alington, once a remarkable headmaster of Eton where he floated about looking saintlike in claret-coloured canonicals, and with him Euclid (what's *he* done to get dropped?), Peter Dawson, the rumbly baritone, Ivor Novello, Van Loon (Dutch historian), Marie Corelli and, to show no snobbish favouritism, the Liberal 8th Duke of Devonshire. The saddest expulsion of all is that of dear old Ethelwulf, our sovereign in 837, who, after 1139 years of glorious prominence, now sinks away into total oblivion.

There are, of course, assorted newcomers—Lord Clark, Paul Robeson, Harold Wilson, and so on, and one of them is really rather unexpected. One shouldn't, I suppose, criticise, and uninvited too, a cyclopaedia's taste, and I dare say that I am old-fashioned, but I do find it rather shaking to discover, on a page which includes W. W. Jacobs, a French loom inventor, Henry James, a Mogul emperor and Amy Johnson, the name of Jesus Christ, just one remove from that of Jerome K. Jerome, who wrote *Three Men in a Boat*. Quite a straightforward entry ('... said to be miraculously conceived... He was later crucified') of 16 lines. Hitler gets 25. Oh well.

ON AVERAGE

Our carefree government has, I observe, been at it again, squandering your and my hard-earned and tax- and VAT-extracted cash. A 'theatre party' has been given (best stalls, I bet, and a box of chocs the size of I don't know what) followed by a simple meal at a snacketeria to which I, the 'man in the street' if ever there was one, don't often get invited and called The Dorchester ('Now, which of you are roast grouse?'). And for whom was this humdrum little outing arranged? Why, 'the Permanent Representatives of the E.E.C.' If they are permanent and can't escape or be changed, whatever can be the point of buttering them so lavishly up? And is there not in this some risk of the modish 'crime' of soft-soaping (and who can say where, in social life, bribery begins or ends?). Or was it just chumminess, and if so why was it at our expense (so easy to be generous with money belonging to others)? Who dares to arrange these expensive treats in the present stony-broke times? The Representatives themselves, chugging happily homeward in, who can doubt, ministerial cars, must now think us even barmier than they did already.

And if they read our newspapers, as I suppose they do, they will find us dottier yet. Item after item convinces me that we are all mad. The Public Record Office, containing matter essential to a vast number and hitherto conveniently situated in Chancery Lane, is, I see, going to go into hiding in Kew. Will it, for good measure, be camouflaged? This, after fifteen years, is what they're up to with those vast duck egg blue domes of the Fylingdales early warning station. This, of course, will hoodwink the Russians entirely when they become either olive green or, and it's not decided yet, a tasteful shade of grey. Meanwhile, a Hammersmith bank-robber arrives to rob in a chauffeur-driven car ('Home, James'), a forest near Nazareth gets itself named after Sir Harold Wilson (and whatever can the trees be? Weeping willows? Sepulchral yews?) and a Northamptonshire sewage works decides to scent the countryside for miles around with heady pine and lemon fragrances. Furthermore, council house tenants, already paying outrageous rents, are not being allowed to get on with their lives in their own normal way. In North Dorset they can't do as they like in their baths. In Oswestry, fleas are out, in Plymouth you aren't welcome to flush empty milk bottles down the lavatory (just what they'd all been hoping to do), while in Exeter neither cats nor dogs are permitted to mate 'without the consent of the housing-officer' ('Hullo, hullo. Is that Mr. Strudwick? I'm afraid Pussy's had a little accident'). I'd like to see bossy Mr. Strudwick trying to explain these restrictive measures at Appleton near Exeter to our spirited little West Highland terrier, Jamie: yap, yap, and a sharp nip in the ankle.

And while we're, temporarily, on oddities, whatever happened about the rummest news item in years, namely that some splendidly new and gleaming tube trains which had been especially designed and built to bring a message of hope and cheer and comfort to those travelling on the Inner Circle were then, bless me, found to be too big to get into the tubes ('Oooops! My tape-measure must have slipped!'). So then they had, expensive work, to lower the tracks to squeeze the jumbos in. Whose fault was it? Was anybody, and do please excuse the verb, sacked? And all these assorted items are brought to us in a joyous cascade of misprints—Dublin has recently been coming out as Lublin, a bride clutching a bouquet of red roses found them to be red noses, while a wretched widow, robbed of her life's savings recklessly stored in a box under her bed, announced in tears to the police that the money represented 'a large bum'.

I pass my life now in a state of total bewilderment. Even my ordinary pleasures conceal mysteries. Who could possibly disagree that the happiest and merriest telly moment of the week is 'Come Dancing'? A fresh and nimble couple twirl themselves lissomely on to the floor, all set for a lively military two-step. 'June's dress', somebody announces, 'is made out of three miles of pink nylon net and she is a costings clerk. Ron is an average-adjuster and they have been engaged for $8\frac{1}{2}$ years. They hope to marry in 1979.' Instant bafflement. We know of what June's evenings consist but what can June's arduous days, costing away like anything, involve? And what, indeed, of Ron, now prancing and gliding down the ballroom floor, white-gloved hand on hip? What possible faith can one have in an average that, day by day, requires adjusting? I referred to myself as the 'man in the street' but on reflection I fear that this is a woefully false claim and so please forget it. Whenever newspapers declare, as they quite frequently do, what the average man is up to, I turn my face to the wall. He, it appears, drinks $3\frac{1}{4}$ pints of beer a week (I don't care for beer). He marries at 22 and has $1\frac{1}{3}$ children (and here I am, still looking keenly about for Miss Right). The other day we were told somewhere the flabbergasting news that the average man's wardrobe was valued at £700 and contained six pairs of jeans. I barely know what jeans are and my wardrobe at 'Myrtlebank' has the ignominious and unusual record of containing items that have been refused, if politely, for parish jumble sales.

When it comes to the yearly average in food and kitchen procedures and meals, I find that I do play my humble part. When dinner comes round, I shall refuse the first course (the average man eats $9\frac{1}{2}$ soused herrings a year, and is welcome to them) but I am all ready for the main dish and a liberal serving of my 184 pounds of meat, two of my 967 potatoes, a sprout or two, and a dollop of my 18 quarts of gravy. And for pudding, part of my 21 bags of suet, and jam from one of my 37 pots. I then wash up and break $4\frac{3}{4}$ plates and use up three of my 532 hiccoughs.

We can now make up our own sad yearly averages before the newspapers arrive at the same figures. Each of us can expect to find $3\frac{1}{3}$ postal items, usually of importance, 'missing'. If we travel by air we can count on being hi-jacked $5\frac{1}{4}$ times. We shall all be burgled $2\frac{2}{3}$ times and mugged $1\frac{1}{2}$. And if we happen to be the wives of foreign embassy officials and we are caught shoplifting in 'a famous store' in Oxford Street, the police will search us and find on us an average of £834.

SUFFER THE LITTLE CHILDREN

As the good Dr. Kissinger continues to flash, like some adult Puck or chunky Shakespearean fairy, now here, now there, over hill, over dale, through African bush and political briar, one is yet again filled with admiration for the remarkable country (and I don't mean Germany) from which he comes. History's pages aren't exactly studded with instances of one nation being helpful, or even polite, to another. Portugal is, as we know, 'our oldest ally', but who ever got a crumb of comfort out of this gossamer relationship? Cynical persons bent on finding unworthy motives in all human behaviour, have had in the past a high old time putting a smear on American post-war generosity. We all know, of course, about the Russian world threat and all that, but it would be agreeable for once to notch up a few votes of thanks from those of us who admire American altruism. It must, I suppose, be purely coincidental that, of all countries, Americans are the most consistently church-going and bible-reading. How very naive of them, but something must have made them what they are. But there, it is fashionable to sneer at the good, though in our Devon village we're so far behind the times that we tend to admire them (odd, too, how catching goodness and kindness are). Smug of us, no doubt.

But away with this Pollyanna mood and cheer up, for I'm moving on to a harsh vote of censure. It is said that anything unfortunate that happens in America (gangsterism, chewing-gum, drugs, Colorado beetles) takes a decade to cross the Atlantic and a further decade for us to become aware of it here, and I suppose it was about ten years ago that we all began to notice that schoolchildren, fresh from the football terraces and full, as like as not, of booze, were busy knifing each other, wrecking telephone kiosks, stealing, tripping up old ladies, and replying to the slightest of reproofs with a pursing of their baby lips and a crisp 'Bugger off!'

I lay much of the blame for this at the feet of America and the deplorable example they have set in the past. Their corporate adoration of children is nauseating and has been so for years. They even find the children's resulting indiscipline in some way engaging and 'cute' ('Why Junior, if you keep kicking Momma's teeth in, Momma is going to have to go get herself a plate'). There must be something parentally unsound in a nation that cooed with idiotic joy when 'the world's sweetheart', Mary Pickford, played (though against her will, but dollars are dollars) Little Lord Fauntleroy at the advanced age of 27 (they made the furniture half as big again, and hired lamp-post-size fellow artistes so that she would appear more wee and appealing). Her golden curls, set on a grown-up frame, had already bobbed their way to fame in a variety of pre-pubic roles—in *Her First Biscuits* (a winsome ten-year-old), *To Save Her Soul* (misled choir girl) and *The Foundling* (a teeny waif). She did *Pollyanna* too. And scarcely was she off American screens than there appeared a dimpled, huggable little mite called Shirley Temple (for years top of the popularity lists and trouncing Garbo and Dietrich). The mischievous rumour that the dimples were held in by suction pads within the little mouth was vigorously denied by the studio.

Anthony Hope, fighting his way out of a performance of *Peter Pan* where the audience had consisted, naturally, chiefly of noisy children, was heard to mutter 'Oh for an hour of Herod!' The shark in 'Jaws' chose, you'll remember, as its second *bonne bouche*, a spoilt and irritating boy who had been annoying his exhausted mother ('Alex, Mom is pooped') on the beach (how delightful, incidentally, the shark looked in the film—a cross between a mini-submarine, off to sink the *Tirpitz*, and a friendly whale with no nutritional objective more elaborate than a *bouchée* of plankton). Though both of these irrevocable means of extermination are possibly going rather far, there is everything to be said for dishing out sharp correctives to children. Married friends of mine, vexed by the frequent and uninvited visits to their bedroom by a young nephew who impertinently ferreted about in their 'things', concealed within them a loaded mousetrap and were soon rewarded by a loud scream of pain as a pink finger-tip got itself pinched. Do please feel free to use this wheeze yourselves. As to brand of mousetrap, for lively work I can personally recommend either 'The Sentinel' or 'The Little Nipper' (advt).

The Victorians, currently despised for their many imperfections, were no slouches when it came to bringing up children. For one thing, families were large and it was dangerous not to crush rebelliousness. And for another, it's clear that, unless they were angelic and preferably rather sickly little girls bound for an early grave, they didn't really like children much. Those who could afford it kept them under by banishing them to nurseries, virtually starving them and scaring the lives out of them by constant reminders of hell and eternal damnation. My mother, born in 1882, was given, as soon as she could read, a book called *The Star of Childhood*, compiled by a priest, and was forced every evening to go through an alarming series of questions ('Have I been obedient?', 'Was I naughty with nurse?', 'What wickednesses have I to confess?') and then had, trembling, to spout out suitable answers.

Earlier on there had been an improving yarn called *The Fairchild Family* by Mrs. Sherwood who, in an autobiography, didn't think it all that odd that in childhood she had been daily strapped into a backboard to aid deportment, lived largely on plain bread and cold milk, and never sat on a chair in her mother's presence. We find a similar absence of *joie de vivre* in the lives of the Fairchild children, Henry, Lucy and Emily. Lucy is caught being envious of Emily's doll and has to pray fervently for forgiveness at her mother's knee. Then Henry is discovered stealing an apple ('Go from my sight, bad boy!') and is locked in an attic. He also prays wildly for forgiveness and gets an hour long pi-jaw from Mr. Fairchild. Then Emily, not to be outdone in naughtiness, steals damsons from the store-cupboard, clumsily souses her knickers in damson juice, gets a frightful chill and hovers for days at death's door, with the family gathered round the bed and praying away like billy-o. And the result of all this tra-la-la? Admirably behaved children—obedient, respectful, thoughtful for others, accepting their lot and only speaking when spoken to. I just thought I'd mention it.

CRYSTAL BALLS

Care to disturb yourself by hearing the latest long-range weather forecast? Very well then. Here goes. 'There will be showers, sometimes heavy, sometimes light, interspersed with clear periods. Slow-moving depressions will move slowly this way and that. Conditions to the east of the Pennines will not be all that dissimilar from what may be expected on the west of the Pennines. Troughs will fill up only when they're good and ready to do so.' There now, that just about covers everything. This forecast comes, not from the Air Ministry roof or the London Weather Centre (with dear Barbara Edwards forcing out a gallant smile at journey's end) but from a quarter that has shown itself to be every bit as reliable. I refer to the bunch of Teignmouth seaweed that hangs here in the hall at 'Myrtlebank', its long tentacle-like brown pennons, when blowing about and seen in a half light, startling impressionable guests out of their wits (they think it's an octopus looking keenly round for its dinner). Its rubbery nodules, now damp, now dry as a bone, have done Trojan service for years and this summer kept pace, completely accurately, with that hottish spell of June, July, August. Further forecasts on request.

The only thing to be said in favour of the future is that we don't, thank God, know what's coming our way though one could safely bet on there being somewhere a bursting cornucopia of assorted nastinesses eagerly waiting to shower its horrid self down on us. The foolhardy and those who can't leave well alone flock to seaside piers and require gypsy-like ladies, sheltering in booths and with barbaric ear-rings jangling and usually called 'Olga', to gaze deep into their crystal contraptions and spill the beans. Their fees are modest enough (there's a small additional charge for reading a sticky palm and announcing excitedly that you're going to get a letter) but the best financial bargain in this sort of field is achieved by the million or so who yearly lay out the sum of 10p in order to discover what Old Moore and his Almanack ('Beware of imitations!') has been able to dream up in the shape of things to come. By way of striking a cheery, comforting note and creating confidence from the start, Mr. Moore (and I can't call him 'Old Moore', which sounds far too familiar a form of address from somebody who was born in 1910 to somebody who was 'founded' in 1697) modestly lists some past forecasting triumphs—the Paris air disaster, the atom bomb on Hiroshima, the Arab oil crisis, the General Strike of 1926, and, for good measure, the Abdication. He doesn't actually mention the Titanic but one senses that all through 1912 he was counselling everybody to stay on dry land.

And don't imagine for a moment that he is running out of disasters. There are plenty more where those came from. When reviewing the future and 1977 month by alarming month, Mr. Moore provides worrying pictorial messages to illustrate and accompany the already sufficiently unsettling text. January alone shows an ominously silent nuclear power station (reactor conked out? Radio-active personnel all gone home? Tea-break?), tanks chugging through burning oil rigs ('Coup in Iraq'), and a terrifyingly violent explosion simply labelled 'NATO'. February is no better—a newspaper placard saying Emergency Powers Possibility (clever Mrs. Thatcher off to a fine start, obviously), a jiggling map of Europe as though in the grip of an earthquake ('Tension'), and a top-hatted City gent squatting grumpily outside some firmly closed doors ('Bank Collapse'). On we go, our spirits sinking—North Sea oil sabotage, widespread strikes, 'India Loses a Leader' (ah!), Belgrade shaking all over, a British delegate getting snubbed by the EEC, widespread flooding, stock market frauds and, just in time for Christmas, 'severe rumblings' (more than likely) coupled with 'Trade Union Funds Scandal'. Nervy, jumpy stuff, as you see, not that Mr. Moore's varied activities in 1697 and the years following were all that calming and peaceful (Death of Racine, War of the Spanish Succession, Blenheim, and the Tory Government of 1710).

By no means all in the 64-page brochure is gloomy prediction. Mr. Moore kindly lets up from time to time and shows an altogether brighter side by popping in some attractive advertisements. We are just trying to recover from the onslaught of Spring when, hey presto, here is The Aquarian Press offering a fine selection of tempting volumes. There is 'Experimental

Magic' (how to contact spirits with the aid of a simple, everyday kitchen implement, and how to 'call cash to you' and then become invisible, two of the handiest imaginable knacks). 'Astral Doorways' encourages faint-hearted old you and stick-in-the-mud me to drag our minds away from Bognor for once and make that astral journey we've been dreaming of for so long, while 'Creative Visualization' announces itself proudly as being an occult technique 'for obtaining all the things you want' which, in my case, would be delivered, I trust, in a plain van. No mysterious jargon to learn, apparently ,'utterly practical' and can be snapped up for a mere £1.95. While lady readers are waiting for their occult techniques to get going ('Drat the thing! I think it's stuck'), they can feast their eyes on the various advertisements for enhancing their attractions and leading to fuller lives—turtle oil cream for smearing on almost anywhere, boxes of 'Vivacity Pills' for that exciting cheese-and-wine 'do' at the Hendersons', and a course of 'Slenderettes' for the body beautiful.

Treading carefully and making full use of the warning phrase 'It is likely that...', Mr. Moore branches out all over the shop—Greyhound Racing Numbers Forecast, lighting-up times for 1977, a list of the principal fairs (for gypsy readers?), where to fish for the best results, and even when the moon is favourable for you to sow your short-topped radishes and, in cosmopolitan mood, your 'Dutch turnips and German greens'. Though one is occasionally baffled by what to me is indeed mysterious jargon ('Saturn moving through Leo to be joined by Mars'), there are up-to-the-minute helpfulnesses on all sides, in particular a section on Inflation and How to Cope with It. Here we divide up into our birth signs. As a Taurean, I find that I have to 'make do with mediocrity for a while' (no surprise, in my case), having already been told that on the very day of my next birthday in May I must 'pay cash for everything' (but, Mr. Moore, dear, are you *mad?*). Also supplied are 'Postal Rates and Information, liable to alteration by the Post Office at short notice'. The thought that they might ever be altered for the better, never even crosses one's mind.

QUIET FLOWS THE DON

A traveller finding himself short of reading matter and trapped overnight in a hotel bedroom in, say, Bournemouth, can always fall back, as it were, on the bible. The splendidly ubiquitous Gideon ('One who cutteth down') Society functions worldwide and as a result of their generosity the good book will be awaiting you expectantly in towns as far apart and as culturally remote from each other as Berlin, Boston and Bude. You will find your bible in the top drawer of the bedside cupboard, where it may also be convenient for you to house your own little personal treasures—teeth, toupee, spectacles, hearing-aid and truss.

Hunting about for remembered episodes, and also hoping to come upon unknown novelties to provide a stimulating bedtime read, one naturally turns, so familiar is the New Testament story, to the Old Testament. Here they all are, those rousing passages that, boomed out in one's youth in a darkening church at Evensong, so seldom lifted the heart.

It will not, I do hope, be thought sacrilegious of me to question the literary abilities of some of the authors. They have a lot to learn in the matter of suspense and many of their chapters don't exactly build to a climax and end with a zing. 'So Mephibosheth dwelt in Jerusalem, for he did eat continuously at the king's table: and was lame on both his feet.' Mephi, who had been dropped as a child, was presumably a distant cousin of poor old Ish-bosheth who, minding his own business and quietly snoozing in his tent, was smitten under the fifth rib and, for good measure, decapitated (Samuel II). Other old favourites and subjects surge up: Heber's wife finding new uses for tent-pegs, the almost morbid keenness on messes of pottage (lentil soup), a warning word about unclean birds (vultures and cuckoos), and that sensational moment when Jezreel's rulers receive a delightful surprise gift from Jehu (70 severed royal heads in an ornamental hamper, a real challenge to Fortnum's).

Fashions in prettiness change, of course, and fairly quickly too (what chance would the solid, statuesque Edwardian beauties, Lily Langtry and Constance Collier, stand today?) and one would hardly expect to find biblical fascinators who could be happily slotted into *Playboy*, but on the other hand the writers' ways of describing them are bizarre indeed. 'Thy navel is like a round goblet, which wanteth not liquor: thy belly is like an heap of wheat set about with lilies.' A gentleman's belly sounds even less practical ('His belly is as bright ivory overlaid with sapphires'). Can attractive eyes have changed all that much? Yes, apparently. 'Thine eyes are like the fishpools in Heshbon.' The association of the word 'fish' with eyes is unfortunate in the extreme. And invariably weird and wonderful are the place names, which would sound quite at home on the lips of a refined and unintelligible English railway station *annonceuse*: 'This is the 10.15 from Joppa, calling at Kinroth-Hattaavah, Michmash, Ziklag, Gilgal and Migdol.'

My friend and undergraduate contemporary, Lionel Gamlin, when editor of the *Granta*, the Cambridge magazine, thought it would be a merry joke to have a parish magazine number, with thoughtful articles by the vicar, reports of sermons ('Last Sunday, Canon Bulmer really let fly on Sodom'), advertisements for cut-price 'Splitproof' copes, and so on. In addition, aware of the 'comfortable words' in the communion service, he thought it would be helpful to supply a disturbing section called 'uncomfortable words', not difficult to run to earth in the Old Testament, with weepings and wailings and gnashings of teeth, threats of plagues and pestilences, and the Maker smiting almost everything in sight. Juvenile fun which, alas, fell dreadfully flat with those in authority and a singularly unsmiling Vice-chancellor (Master of Magdalene) summoned the editor and gave him a frightful time. Lionel could well have put up a spirited defence (he hadn't been President of the Union for nothing) but decided that humble contrition and a hearty show of repentance were the advisable thing and, by so doing, avoided being sent down.

He might have fared better with a previous Master of Magdalene who had considerably more understanding of youthful high spirits, despite a rather ponderous side to his character. If the Gideon Society were ever to consider distributing further reputable material as a soporific bedside alternative to the excitements of the Old Testament, they might do worse than to delve into the collected works of a considerable figure, Arthur Benson. Archbishop Benson, the first Master of Wellington College and subsequently resident at Canterbury, sired four gifted sons, one of them, Arthur, moving, after many successful years as an Eton master, to Cambridge in 1905. There he toiled ceaselessly and profitably by day on behalf of the college, but, as evening approached, there came the 'sacred hours' when he locked himself in his rooms and his self-indulgent thoughts and prosaic opinions flowed with a fatal fluency over endless sheets of paper. His three main subjects were the beauty of Nature, of the countryside in general, and of God in particular. Like Shakespeare, he never blotted out a line, and more's the pity.

The titles of the hugely popular volumes that resulted from this daily activity speak for themselves (*Beside Still Waters, Thy Rod and Thy Staff, The Altar Fire,* etc.) and all are imbued with guidance and uplift, with everywhere the Divine Hand present. Indeed, 'I think that God has put it into my heart to write this book.' Well, this may have been so but one must add that God, as co-author, had unfortunately decided to leave both his thunderbolts and his sense of humour in the cloakroom.

Here is indeed a vanished age and attitude. All is peace, perfect peace. The effortless ramblings tell of stone dove-cots, balmy winds, birds melodiously fluting, cows mooing ('They bring a deep tranquillity into the spirit'), the joys of self-denial, gnarled gardeners feverishly humming Rock of Ages, gracious people 'in comely apparel', gently-swelling downlands, all summed up in the phrase 'It is England—tranquil, healthy, prosperous England.'

Is there, then, no fly in the ointment? Yes, alas. The author is apt to complain of the way in which the less fortunate just don't seem to notice beauty. 'I wish with all my heart that all classes cared equally for the things which I love', he muses, possibly munching another buttery muffin, 'but I find that the lower classes are not interested in these things.' Too bad of them, but they had, perhaps, other preoccupations. Poverty and hunger, for instance.

DOWN THE RED LANE

Whatever can be the opposite, *je me demande* from time to time, of *bon viveur*? Obviously not *mauvais viveur* but what, to a French ear, would imply the simple life and holding back at the table? *Viveur limité* perhaps, or possibly *viveur peu distingué*? At all events, it is the *bon* kind that concerns us here and the *Daily Telegraph*, ever mindful of what is best, the *crème de la crème* in fact, in modern journalism, keeps us posted weekly on the calorie-packed munchings of those delightful Cradocks, nobly risking coronaries on our behalf as they traipse about the country and the continent sampling, here an avocado mousse with 'wet-fresh' Morecambe Bay prawns and chicken's livers cooked with cream, mushrooms and marjoram, there *crevette vol-au-vents* with 'exquisite *feuilletage*' and, to wind up, fluted brandy-snap cases crammed with ginger cream. The Cradocks revel, and why not, in their happy guzzlings and our mouths water with them.

I am all in favour of this frankness about food being extended. It would help greatly to understand people and their quaint ways if only we knew what, say, they had had for breakfast. Perhaps when notabilities appear on the telly, we could, in addition to having their names faded in and faded out beneath their faces, have details of the most recent meal they have consumed—'Steak and kidney pie. Cabinet pudding.' or 'On a diet. Rollmops', the latter fully explaining the sour expression and bitter views. Everybody knows that after a grilled kipper at 8.30 a.m. the rest of the day goes with a merry zing. It seems extremely likely that on the day that, in a state of unbridled *joie de vivre*, Mr. Healey spoke exultantly of the non-existent 'economic miracle', Mrs. Healey had recklessly provided him with a grilled kipper. Perhaps, for one cannot imagine that in a government-run establishment in Downing Street there is any sort of stint or cheese-paring, Mr. Healey ate *two* disastrous kippers, a fatal intake. If it had to be fish, Mrs. Healey would have been wise to construct some home-made fish-cakes with double the normal potato content. This humble, filling dish would have damped him down and spared us the shock and disappointment of discovering, after being incorrectly told that all was well, that all was lousy. Bland and calming foods are what the Chancellor must have from now on in, or now on out as the case may be.

And in this connection our thoughts now fly across the Atlantic and to the day when chunky President Ford, in dream-o'-day-Jill mood, told us how enormously contented and free to do as they wish are all countries beyond the Iron Curtain. Happy as larks they are, oh yes indeedy. Now what on earth can Mrs. Ford have provided for breakfast on that unfortunate day? President Ford has, I would think, a sluggish digestion requiring a goodish bit of roughage. There would have been ice-cold orange-juice, of course, and then I can, sad to say, see him going a bit too hard at the soggy waffles, two words which in this context are all too apposite. Here was a case, if ever there was one, of sharpening him with a grilled kipper. Are there kippers in Washington? Perhaps Mrs. Armstrong could pop a few into the diplomatic bag.

In the field of literature, information about food would be extremely valuable. I have complained before about how little of importance authors deign to tell us of their characters. To hell with what's going on in their minds, it's what's happening in their midriffs that really matters. Take Ophelia. Millais' famous portrait of her drowned, flower-strewn corpse has done a great disservice to historical fact. As we know, he used as a model a beautiful milliner's assistant, Elizabeth Siddal, tall and slender with a swanlike neck and a delicate physique, a physique which he made even more delicate by popping her, fully clothed, into his bath in Gower Street and then floating her about, vigorously painting, while the water grew ever colder. The true facts are quite otherwise. Ophelia was in no way listless or lifeless but a strong, sturdy girl who, finding herself immersed in a brook, would have waded to the bank in a trice. In any case, the streams in the neighbourhood of Elsinore are notoriously feeble, mere trickles and knee-deep at the best. Danish butter and bacon are among the world's finest and, reared in pampered conditions at the Danish court, Ophelia would have eaten only of the best and developed a robust constitution. Her intimate knowledge of wild flowers and herbs argues a *cuisine raffinée*, supervised by her mother, a somewhat shadowy and withdrawn figure.

There is the further evidence of Laertes, brought up in the same household. Nobody can duel or leap nimbly into graves on an empty stomach and Laertes's fine display of swordsmanship can only have come from a background where good food, and the doughty bones and sinews that it produces, was fully understood. But how then did Ophelia die? It is perfectly clear. Danish bacon, ergo Danish pork chops, a meat which takes a long time to digest. Ophelia, taking a quick dip after lunch on a sultry afternoon, failed to allow the precautionary 1½ hours rest after a heavy meal (she would have topped up with a Danish pastry or two) and was struck down by Bürger's Disease (violent spasms in the arteries). Because it suited his book, Shakespeare deliberately concealed the facts, not for the first or last time.

But if only we knew. I tend to feel that elegant Mrs. Thatcher has no breakfast (just some fragrant Earl Grey perhaps) but makes quite a 'thing' of tea, with a cooked dish or two, Welsh rarebit perhaps, or some of clever Zena Skinner's 'crispy bacon bites' and a generous pile of 'peel and almond cookies'. Then a quick dash, fortified and with charming smile in position, to the House. *Private Eye* used to give us some inkling, right or wrong, of what the Wilsons ate, but has anybody any idea at all of what goes down the red lane in the Callaghan family? Apart from Lord Home, the diet of Prime Ministers of recent years has obviously not been starch-free. Mr. Heath increasingly presented the bonniest of aspects, and very nice too. Is Mrs. Shirley Williams (being groomed for stardom, I trust) getting enough protein? Her brains, and they are good ones, need it. One worries about these things.

Until recent years, the eating habits of royalty have been a mystery. The facts are meagre. We know what Charles Laughton so untidily ate as Henry VIII, and we know that Edward VII ate anything and everything. Apart from the wailing cry of 'No pudding, no fun', Queen Victoria is above such mundane matters in her Journal, though Albert's taxing marital duties must, heaven knows, have required some pretty solid stuff. I say 'until recent years' because a splendid lady called Mrs. McKee, cook to royalty, was persuaded a few years ago to draw back the curtain a little and tell us what was considered toothsome in Buckingham Palace, Clarence House, Balmoral and so on. Mrs. McKee, born in Sweden, is naturally strong on smörgasbord and nettle soup with egg balls and, alas, soused mackerel, but is in general game for anything and flinches at nothing—mousse of lychees, eggs in curried mayonnaise, stuffed braised cucumber, rice croquettes with pineapple sauce, cold cherry soup Cantilly. Concerning who likes what, Mrs. McKee is the soul of tact but reading between the lines one senses that the Queen Mother's tastes are for the fortifying coupled with the exotic (hot grapefruit salad with the roast duckling and consommé dotted with *bouchées mimosa*, a sustaining combination of pastry, parmesan, truffles, eggs and about a quart of cream). Those who marvel at Her Majesty The Queen's trim figure can take comfort from the fact that she is by no means a stranger to spuds and tucked in, in younger days, to banana-filled meringues in candied syrup. Princess Margaret, on the other hand, has always been, we learn, especially fond of hot soup.

ALL WRONG ON THE NIGHT

This is the joyous period of the year when, with the dreaded exams approaching their climax and the end of term more or less in sight, school halls and assembly rooms are being put temporarily out of bounds while workmen and staff labour to erect stages from trestles, planks, tables, benches or whatever, stages on which home-made entertainments of assorted kinds are to take place—school plays, concerts, variety evenings, sing-songs and so on.

For almost all of my long life I have been merrily involved with amateur entertainments of, frequently, the most desperately incompetent kind. There is nothing in the way of beetroot make-ups and George Robey eyebrows, forgotten lines, collapsing scenery, missed entrances, fluffed lines and general theatrical mishaps that would come to me in the smallest way as a surprise. Among other things, I know all about those rather grubby tights that are found, and at the very last moment, to have split ('But Donald, you *can't* go on like that. Everything's showing').

I kicked off early, aged nine, at my prep school on the Hampshire coast. Here it was the custom to celebrate the end of the summer term by treating the parents and any local residents who hadn't attended one before (silver collection in aid of Dr. Barnardo) to an entertainment provided jointly by the school staff and boys. The music mistress, gifted Mrs. Wakefield, a resplendent figure in coffee lace, was perched at the upright, candles in holders illuminating her music, and got us off to a fine start with a tuneful selection from *The Gondoliers*, with much fancy fingering and elaborate crossing of the arms.

Then, to a jerky rattling of curtain-rings, the curtains parted to reveal four alarmed treble singers, nearly blinded by the bright, tin-encased footlights and who, by ancient usage, gave us what was always described as 'a traditional English air', quite often 'Early One Morning':

Early one mor-hor-ning
Just as the sun was ri-hi-sing

they warbled, Mrs. Wakefield, all smiles, helpfully thundering out the melody.

With that safely, more or less, out of the way, our hearts sank. Again by old custom, item No. 2 featured the sports master, genial Captain Murray, in a baritone solo. For the four years that I was at the school, his song was the same. It told of the open road and the fine free life of the wayfaring pedestrian. I forget both name and composer but it started spiritedly:

When you're jog-jog-jogging along the high road
With your luck all upside down.

Nobody could have jog-jog-jogged more cheerfully than Captain Murray. For this melodious piece he wore tattered corduroy trousers supported by a leather belt and became, in a trice, the very epitome of carefree tramphood. With legs well apart and a thumb tucked into the waistband of the bags, he was, pictorially, the school's defiant answer to Peter Dawson. But there it ended. There was no trace of Peter Dawson's splendid rumblings about the Captain's voice. It was thin and scratchy and quite tremendously off key. The more musical boys winced and even Mrs. Wakefield, the personification of loyalty, wore a strained look. I longed, though in vain, for him to do well (he had been gassed in the war, which shows which dreadful war it was) and I violently led the applause, anxious about my own dramatic contribution that was to come later.

One summer term, Matron electrified the entire school by coyly announcing that, if we would really and truly like her to, she would recite a poem which she referred to as 'The Daffodils'. 'By Wordsworth,' she added, a positive mine of cultured information. She had 'done' it as a girl and had now refreshed her memory and was only too delighted to pronounce herself as being word perfect.

Her offer was, naturally, gratefully accepted. One had never dreamt that such virtuosity would emerge from behind that crackling white starch, which normally only dispensed iodine, zinc ointment, lint, bracing talk ('I've had quite enough of your nonsense') and Gregory powder, which always sounded to me like a wealthy industrialist ('... and now I will ask our chairman,

Sir Gregory Powder, to make his annual report'—rather a loud bang, I imagine).

With cries of 'No, no, I shall wait for The Night', Matron refused to reveal her powers at any rehearsal, and so, with Captain Murray's last despairing wails ('There's no luck waiting along the high road for a vagabond like me') still echoing round the hall, Matron, impressive in mufti, made her stately appearance.

I only wish that I could report a dazzling triumph, with the local paper, the *Gosport Sentinel*, describing her as 'a second Siddons' but it was no such thing. She began quite well and certainly wandered lonely as a cloud that floats on high o'er vales and hills. She got through the milky way section and seemed all set for booming out the finale but after 'For oft, when on my couch I lie', disaster struck. Her voice trailed despairingly off and she dried up completely. Of course, in those days we didn't call it 'drying up'. 'Matron's stopped speaking' we said. Pluckily, but how unwisely, she started all over again, evidently with some idea of getting a fresh run at the thing and bridging the gap. She wandered lonely as a cloud once more, only to come adrift again upon her couch. The headmaster tactfully led loud applause, Matron had the nerve to take a bow, and the curtains rattled mercifully to.

By dint of being generally odious, whining all day long and ceaselessly badgering poor Mr. Riches, our compère, I had secured for myself a solo appearance. My passion to display myself was quite unbridled and so Mr. Riches kindly sent up to Samuel French for a suitable recitation and back one duly came. It was entitled 'The Single Hair' and described itself as a Comic Monologue. To this day I can, heaven help me, remember every word of it (a shining example to Matron). It began with a strong comedic couplet:

He was not bald, for on his shining cranium
Remained one hair, its colour pink geranium.

After several more equally hilarious couplets, the hair falls off (into his soup), is rescued and a taxidermist is called in. And so to the pay-off:

And stuffed, within its case of glass installed,
It shows the world, HE WAS NOT ALWAYS BALD.

To utter this risible gem, I was dressed in pierrot costume and the applause was tumultuous. Even today, I sometimes in dreams deliver the piece again and frighten myself awake, sweating with the appalling horror of it all.

In the field of more adult school entertainments, the scope for imperfections is altogether wider, especially in Shakespeare. Julius Caesar, on that unfortunate visit to the Senate-house, is sometimes seen to have prudently retained his wrist-watch, thus enabling Mark Antony, at the subsequent enquiry, to fix with reasonable accuracy the time of the crime. I have seen a Lady Macbeth, evidently keenly following the text while in the wings, make her entrance for the sleep-walking scene wearing a large pair of horn-rimmed spectacles. I have been there when the dead body of Hamlet, which had been lying for some moments upon a rather dusty stage, had been shaken by a shattering succession of sneezes, somewhat spoiling Horatio's soulful rendering of 'Now cracks a noble heart'.

In isolated schools which have to rely on their own resources, girls have to appear as boys and boys as girls. In the latter case, and to aid the illusion, housemasters' wives used kindly to construct false bosoms from pads of cotton wool of strictly modest dimensions. These were known to us as 'shapes' ('Please, Mrs. Henderson, we're going to need three more shapes'). They were then safety-pinned to vests and, in the exertions of the performance, sometimes either came unhitched and fell off or ended up in unusual positions. And in addition to bulging strangely, it was often far from easy for performers to leave the stage. The doors in the insecurely-roped-together 'flats' which formed the boxed-in set gave no indication as to whether they had to be pushed or pulled. It was fatally easy to utter a dramatic exit line and then ruin all by pushing instead of pulling, while the scenery swayed dangerously and those in the front rows looked anxiously about for the nearest exit.

Most perilous of all are entertainments out of doors—Greek plays rendered inaudible by high winds and Jumbo jets passing overhead, or vast historical pageants when every brush and shrub for miles around is alive with agitated middle-aged ladies frenziedly dressing up as somebody else ('Cynthia dear, what have you done with my whimple?'). Pageants invariably require horses, and horses have little or no idea of what constitutes appropriate public behaviour.

Even in the professional theatre, anything out of doors is risky. I once attended, a glutton for punishment, an extremely under-rehearsed performance of A *Midsummer Night's Dream* in a public park. An orchestra, concealed behind a privet hedge, scraped away at Mendelssohn's music and there was a good bit of dancing, with fairies fluttering hither and thither. In due course they made their exit, gossamer wings a-flapping, down a gravel path and disappeared round a corner, only to reappear again soon after, in some disarray and flapping more violently than ever. It later transpired that they had mistakenly exited full tilt into the Gentlemen's Lavatory from which they had, rightly, been at once ejected.

IN AT THE SHALLOW END

A crusty old bachelor such as myself, aged 66 and living in a Devon backwater, can hardly be expected to know anything of Life, if our kind printer will permit me a capital, or sex or where babies come from and so, before the sands run out and the grim reaper scythes me down, I'm considering boning up on these agitating subjects. Alarmed readers need not give a gasp and stop reading here. I'm as nervous as you are. We're in this together and we'll proceed carefully. Aware that matters such as this must be studied from both the practical and theoretical sides, I see myself in my mind's eye boldly applying to a 'computer-dating service' and, after answering a number of impertinent questions and enclosing a fiver, a sharp rat-tat-tat at my door at 4 p.m. brings my electronically-selected 'date'. A Miss E. Bagshaw, 48 if a day, in a Henry Heath hat and fawn tailor-made. Shod with stout brogues, she has the general appearance of a lady golfer of the 1930s about to take a swipe at the dog-leg hole at Sunningdale. Not exactly a *troublante* figure but one has to start somewhere, I suppose.

With my practical experiment all set up on the sofa and ready to go, I turn to the theoretical side, and here I have had a bit of luck. Applying shyly for help from our charming NS literary editress, she thrust into my hand the two-volumed paperback edition of John Atkins's invaluable *Sex in Literature*, published in hardback a few years ago and a mine of useful information at all times, the 'Literature' part of the title conferring a scholarly respectability on some of the rum goings-on within. The moment the judge and jury were informed by cultured witnesses that *Lady Chatterley's Lover* was 'Literature', there wasn't a hope of getting it banned. If it's Eng. Lit., anything goes.

Anyhow, I've now read the book and there before me sits Miss Bagshaw. I see myself breaking the ice with an offer of tea, no wishy-washy Chinese kind but a strongish brew of the best Darjeeling (one spoonful for me, one for Miss Bagshaw, and one for the pot) and, as a subtle, tactful compliment to my fair visitor, sandwiches filled with Gentlemen's Relish. And now, after this treat, how to kick off? Perhaps I should make a strong beginning with the old Mau Mau courting custom of forming on the floor a circle of banana leaves, potatoes, sugar cane and molasses and requesting Miss Bagshaw to step into the middle of it and take all her clothes off. She should then squat down and eat some unusual parts of a dead ram which, though no doubt tasty and calorie-packed, would not be immediately obtainable, unless previously ordered, from our local butcher. Possibly this perfectly simple request is rather too elaborate for starters, and anyhow, bananas, either leaves or fruit, are perilous material, Malayan pygmies, who must have very vivid minds, considering it indecent to eat a banana in public. And meanwhile I wonder what that 'E' stands for. Ethel? Edythe?

Any thought of getting amatory inspiration from modern Russian novels must be at once abandoned. The Communists do not care for erotic themes or treatment because of their emphasis on the individual. Authors have to be wary of love's fulfilments. In the post-war best-seller, *Far From Moscow*, a sober couple called Mikhail and Tanya are in love and happily find themselves alone in the house of Tanya's parents, but Tanya spoils everything by suddenly developing nettle rash and Mikhail has to rub her legs with alcohol. I can hardly ask Miss Bagshaw whether she has nettle rash and then souse her legs with Smirnoff. We certainly have some nettles in the orchard and later on I might lead her through them and see what happens. In Tanya's case she merely got even moodier than before.

Remembering the old saying, 'When gentlefolk meet, compliments fly', I could fire off a few politenesses at Miss B and here one turns for assistance confidently to Syria and a wedding-feast panegyric from the flowery pen of Kasim al Chinn: 'Your neck is like the neck of a roe, your legs are marble pillars in the sacred house of the Omayads, your arms are peeled cucumbers', (well, that's what it says), 'your body is a mass of cotton-wool and your navel is so deep that it would hold an ounce of nutmeg butter.' Perhaps, when it comes to it, I'll re-word those compliments a little, the combination of the words marble, cucumber, cotton-wool and nutmeg butter providing rather a baffling picture.

If only we were living in the eighteenth century I wouldn't be put to all this trouble. I could join a 'love club' called the Aphrodites, open to both sexes, with a membership fee of £10,000 (no reduction for country members). The journal of a lady member has been preserved and reveals that in twenty years she rubbed friendly shoulders with 420 'society men', 929 officers, 439 monks, 117 valets, 93 rabbis, 119 musicians, 1614 foreigners, 12 cousins and 2 uncles.

Sir R. F. Burton, playing with fire when translating interesting Arabian works, was really on to something helpful with the *Kama Sutra*'s section on kissing. Here's variety! Ordinary kisses come in six kinds, the straight, the limited, the oblique (screw the face round sideways and form the lower lip into an O), the exploratory, the revolving (seize your partner's head and chin and revolve them briskly), and the cupping, which if properly carried out should result in a loud whistling sound (hopeless to attempt it if either of you has a moustache). For advanced students there are the diverting (aimed at stopping a man dropping off to sleep), the worshipful (chastely planted on the draped bosom) and the signalling ('which shows desire when returning home late'). If a lady, while helping a gentleman out of his clothes, should choose to peck his big toe, this is called the demonstrative kiss. I'll say. And in *The Golden Lotus* there are some excellent tips (cinnamon tablets, aromatic tea) for ensuring tingling mouth freshness.

But good heavens, what is this? 6 p.m. and Miss Bagshaw is gathering up her 'things' and preparing to leave, with nothing achieved. Oh well, better luck next time, though actually I'm rather inclined to leave things there. But if you would care to have a go, Calder & Boyars sell the books at £2.95 each, and worth every new p.

HAPPY DAYS

Maurice Bowra was a great collector and hoarder of any information, however tenuous, concerning scholastic matters and if, in my wanderings by car to and fro across the country, I found myself near a public school, he liked me to send him a short report on the current 'tone' of the place. The way to discover what the 'tone' is like is to linger, as though absorbed in the beauty of the ancient buildings (and here quite a feat of mime is sometimes required), near a knot of chattering schoolboys, keep your ears open, and test for 'tone'. In this way, I was able to supply him with up-to-the-minute news on Shrewsbury (excellent), Sherborne (saintly), Uppingham (a tendency to harp on cricket but otherwise admirable), Harrow (faultless), his old school, Cheltenham (all that one could wish) and a few others where, alas, the 'tone' seemed to have slipped a bit. All my bulletins were, of course, acknowledged in a characteristic manner ('Just as I thought! Poor old Cloggers has let the place go to pot. I shall advise *everybody* to give it a miss'), and now that he has gone, there is no central point where I can send any further information that may come my way.

Something tells me that in years to come we're going to be a bit short on public school facts of the more interesting and personal, human kind. Past autobiographers, smarting from remembered grudges and the rigours of the tough life, used to pour out their anguished souls to us in volume after volume. But in the last twenty years or so, life in such schools has radically changed for the better and there is now little in the way of grudges or unhappinesses to force out the tortured words. By and large, bullying and beating are out, and fagging on the way so. Boys in their last year are treated more as undergraduates. It is possible to question, politely, the decisions of authority. Co-education helps with some of the tricky amatory problems. Freedom (beer evenings: dances) is in the air. There is much less compulsory religion and team-games are no longer all-important. In some establishments, there is even Sunday breakfast in bed (oh yes, though they have to fetch it themselves). Nothing really, as you see, to moan and groan about.

Past moaners and groaners have included many distinguished literary figures, and though all complain, the higher they subsequently got up achievement's ladder, the more they were inclined to treat the whole bizarre public school life not in just a sour, disgruntled manner but as a splendid joke. Siegfried Sassoon, known at Marlborough as either 'Stinkweed Bassoon' or 'Seaweed Baboon', take your pick, was called 'The Onion' at his prep school, the name subtly implying that he was off his onion. At the memorial service for Queen Victoria, an assistant master cheered up the solemn, lachrymose occasion by sitting down on his bowler hat and squashing it flat. Superannuated at the age of 17, he had the distinction of being prayed for in Chapel (double pneumonia) and winning a half-crown prize for some *vers d'occasion*:

> But extra lessons cannot kill,
> And blows are not so hard
> That they will end the life of this
> Ambitious little bard.

In all, it had been 'an educational experience that I found moderately pleasant but mentally unprofitable.'

Graham Robertson, coming from an austere prep school where every waking thought revolved round Thursdays (sausage morning), found at Eton much that was entertaining, in particular the card announcing the Anthems for the day together with the names of the composers and which, containing no punctuation, read strangely: 'Sing unto the Lord a new song George Macfarren' and 'Wash me thoroughly Joseph Barnby'. And he was lucky enough to coincide with a craze for aviation by mice in parachutes which, one summer term, was all the rage. The boys, loath to kill the little creatures that swarmed in their rooms, fashioned aerial contraptions, complete with seating accommodation, and floated the mice down from upper windows and into neighbouring gardens, where the passengers were able to alight and make off. Once, on a day of boisterous wind, an aeronaut was carried further afield than usual and came sailing through an open window and into a master's tea-party, where the sudden appearance of a mouse comfortably seated in a parachute was considered to be a deliberate insult.

Headmasters, then often autocratic dictators beyond the reach of both humanity and the law, frequently spread terror. Robertson Scott's grammar school one had a habit, riveting for children, of thrusting his beard into his mouth, mumbling it for a moment or two, and then ferociously blowing it out again with a loud 'pop'. When mounting furies became too much for him, he would rush to his wife who, with a bucket of cold water ever at the ready, would damp him down by pouring it over his head (it is no surprise to learn that his life went somehow agley and he wound up, perfectly contentedly, as a clerk in a laundry). At Lord Berners' prep school, where the days passed by against a permanent background of muffled sobbing, there was the terrifyingly sadistic Mr. Gambril who lifted boys into the air by their hair and nearly had apoplexy when he discovered that the school's keen biologists, who collected beetles, caterpillars and insects and were known as 'bug-hunters', had conveniently and innocently contracted their name and called themselves 'buggers'. When Lord Berners, many years later, returned to visit the school he was astonished to observe nothing but smiling faces and peaceful happiness everywhere, only to find that it was a school no more and that the buildings were now a lunatic asylum. At G. G. Coulton's school, Felsted, the alarming but conscientious headmaster, dutifully attending an O.T.C. Field Day, had his tall silk hat blown off into a hedge by prematurely exploding blanks, in the same week as the arrival of a new French master who, reporting for duty on a Saturday night, was found on Sunday morning dead-drunk in a pigsty behind the chapel.

Edward Marsh, bright as a button, mastered at his London day-school the ten commandments and, somewhat baffled by the seventh (if you're rusty, adultery) and anxious to discover its meaning, put a question to the headmistress, Miss Scripps, who replied briskly that it meant that we must none of us over-eat ourselves. Passing on to Westminster, he was mysteriously and unjustly given an impot for laughing in class at a passage from Molière, and joined in the typical schoolboy giggles when the headmaster, discussing Alison's *History of Europe*, loudly intoned a sentence which went 'The Austrians held the Po, while the Italians slowly evacuated.' Least of all would one have wished to be at Richard Church's Battersea school where the headmaster, a pince-nezed ungenial giant who wore spats all the year round, sat enthroned before an open chest containing a sort of golf-bag assortment of what advertisements for school equipment used to call 'young gentlemen's correction switches'—some thin, some thick, some light in colour and some unaccountably dark, as though impregnated with blood. Boys summoned for punishment toed a white line and waited, trembling, for minutes on end, sometimes standing in little pools of anxious water. How very cheering to learn that one spirited boy revolted and, with an hysterical cry, flung an ink-pot at the tyrant, scoring a splendid bull's-eye.

When my Uncle Oswald was going in 1908 as a scholar (the only brains of the family, as is clear) to Rugby, my grandfather, agitated about his well-being, wisely purchased *Health At School*, a thoughtful work by the school doctor, Clement Dukes, and dedicated to Arnold. Helpful illustrations and charts abound —'Archer's Water-tight Sewer Pipe', 'How to Sit at the Pianoforte', 'A School Grease-trap in Operation', 'Average Heights and Weights of the Most Favoured Classes' (a comparison with the 'Artisan' class shows the latter to be somewhat shorter and lighter. Odd). Information on how, at Rugby, they resuscitated the drowning, and the mortality rate from measles, can hardly have spread confidence, and when deciding which Comprehensive to choose for Jason and Melissa, follow Dr. Dukes and do keep right on your toes. A child with gouty parents should have a hilltop school facing south and planted firmly on gravel. Rheumaticky subjects should beware of clay. Where there is insanity in the family, avoid all cramming for exams. Demand from the headmaster full details of his subsoil drainage, his water levels, his proximity to an alluvial plain (*not* recommended), and the proportion of clerical to lay masters (1 to 6 is just about right). Is the matron suitably elderly? Is it realised what hot baths *at night* may lead to? Has the school installed an earth closet 'as suggested and devised by the Rev. Henry Moule', presumably during a momentary absence from the pulpit? And on no account be put off by evasive answers.

OFF MY CHEST

I seldom, as you know, complain, but until recent years I do seem to have spent rather big chunks of my life with people who, with minimal justification, became rather frequently ratty (ever since that nice Mr. Dubrovsky started translating me into Russian I've been anxious about my adjectives: whatever would 'ratty' come out as?). Nice enough people, too, but every now and then cross-patch. Sulky and impervious ('Oh I say, *do* cheer up!') to encouragements. Grumpy and keen to remain so. And so busy being huffy that I've never been allowed any time myself to be huffy too. So now I do really feel that it is my turn and I've got three things that I feel fairly ratty about.

I've mentioned before our total lack of leadership and the drought has revealed leadership at its nadir. Is there a government governing somewhere? One would hardly think so. Weeks, if not months, ago, all television and radio should have been halted at 9 p.m. (or, preferably, in the middle of *It's A Knockout*, possibly the most humanly degrading and profitless programme ever dreamt up) for a special announcement. Then the Prime Minister, and goodness me how difficult it is to remember which of those ambitious nonentities we finally got landed with, could, grim-faced, have popped up on the box and given it to us straight. Properly put over and explained, water consumption could, six weeks ago, have been cut by half. We could then have panned, as we say in the telly studios, to the Archbishop of Canterbury who, with a breathy selection of devout prayers, could have tried out his abilities as a rain-maker.

The government seems unaware that, in the British people and their strange attitude to life, they are sitting on a mine of untapped goodwill and endeavour. Disasters, potential or real, only serve to keep us happy and on our toes. In 1940 the information that things were bad and were going to become appalling, was received with nothing but joyous enthusiasm. Horrors stimulate and cheer us and give us the will to press on. It is significant that Sweden, a country to which nothing of the remotest interest has ever happened, has the highest suicide rate in the world.

And now on to the National Theatre, and not concerning its mechanised and computerised scenic wonders (gone totally wonky, I hear), or what is now called its visual impact (outstandingly hideous), but the names of the three auditoria. 'Olivier' for one is very right and proper, but why not 'Gielgud' and 'Evans' for the others, two blazing talents which also deserve recognition? Names which mean nothing to the public are merely idiotic and I am reminded of a day in 1944 when, to help celebrate the liberation of Paris, Grace Moore kindly consented to sing there. An aeroplane flew over the city scattering leaflets which fluttered down and said '*Grace Moore chantera ce soir du balcon de l'Opéra*'. The French, who for years had had the Germans on their backs and the occupation on their minds, had no idea who she was. They stared at the leaflets bewildered, muttering 'Qui est cette Grace Moore?'. Well, qui est ce Cottesloe? Qui ce Lyttelton? They have plainly done splendid work on the project, and their names are household to a small circle, I don't doubt, but that is all. In twenty years' time they will be a mystery. And why surnames at all? Why not, say, 'The Open Theatre', 'The Proscenium Theatre', and 'The Small Theatre' so that we know more or less what we are in for? But will anything be changed? Oh dear me no. Being what we are, the hopelessness and complete inadequacy of the names chosen ensures them a very long life. Incidentally, did the gentlemen concerned blushingly agree? Whose decision was it? What exactly went on?

And so to my last bit of grumpiness. It's quite simple. It's just that I'm fed up with books about Jack the Ripper. Down the years they've been coming in as though on a conveyor-belt. Two appeared in 1965 and one thought that must really be all, but no. Two more have emerged, jammed with the usual doubts and speculations. The possibilities as to the Ripper's identity are endless—a Broadmoor fetishist suitably called Cutbush, a Winchester Prefect of Chapel, a Jewish ritual slaughterman, and so on. Two suggestions, namely that it was either a woman or that it was Prince Eddy, Duke of Clarence, close to the throne and engaged to Princess May of Teck, are so near to the truth that they have decided me to speak out at last. I have here at 'Myrtlebank' conclusive evidence of a startling kind that puts the matter for ever beyond all doubt.

It is a diary kept by my great-grandmother, Florence Marshall, the 'dramatic *monologuiste*' who spouted histrionically in Victorian drawing-rooms for a substantial fee (her 'Joan at the Stake' was said to be very fine) and whose stage name was Caresse de Bathe. The combination of the respected surname, her talent and her commanding presence wafted her into social circles well beyond my family's normal reach and we have since, as you see, sunk back ('Myrtlebank'! I ask you!). Billed up and down the country as 'the great diseuse', a word which mischievous schoolboys found it only too easy to change to 'disease', she spent much of her time in London, as her diary shows:

> To White Lodge to tea with the Tecks (the Duchess *enormous*) where Princess May joined us, just back from her voluntary duties in the surgical ward at Bart's and full of excitement. She goes quite often.

From then on, the rest is clear and one can see it all—the engagement to the weak and dissipated Prince, his confiding to her of his secret, murderous longings, the cry of 'No, no' from the distraught Princess, and then her brave decision to let her adored fiancé enjoy himself by proxy. Then the concealment of various useful surgical instruments from Bart's, a scalpel here, a hack-saw there (under those voluminous Victorian clothes you could have hidden a kitchen range and grilled a kidney without anybody being any the wiser). And so to the fatal nights, five in all, with the excuses ('I shall be late home, Mama, we're amputating'), the hurried cab drives to Whitechapel, the hasty despatch of victim after victim, the return to White Lodge, the sponging and the dabbing and the rush to Marlborough House for breakfast with Eddy ('More kedgeree, dear?') while, firm as Lady Macbeth, she poured out every ghoulish detail. Yes, yes. It is quite obvious. *Jack the Ripper was Queen Mary.* And now please don't let us hear another word about the whole ridiculous and time-wasting business.

THERE GO YOUR PIPS

Long distance telephoning is nowadays a commonplace, everyday matter and about as exciting as cleaning your teeth. A brief glance at the code-book, a deft twiddling of the dial and there you are, jabbering away nineteen to the dozen to friends in Fiji. But in the pre-dialling days of local and central switchboards, manned mainly by female operators with diplomas in elocution, making a call was what the French so graphically term *toute une affaire* and at no time more so than at Christmas, when the elocutionists were run off their feet. Then the urge to speak to loved ones and relations (not always the same thing) became irresistible. Throughout Christmas week houses rang with shrieks of 'What's Aunt Honor's number?' and 'No answer! She's probably out at a mah-jongg party'. Sometimes, particularly in Surrey, the telephone apparatus itself was concealed beneath the skirts of a dainty little telephone lady in a crinoline, a saucy idea which possibly brought a *frisson* to tired, male, stockbroking loins, but more often than not the instrument was on a bracket on a wall near the front door and from it jolly Uncle Bob in Darlington got his yearly call ('How's that old leg of yours?'). Game old grannies were carefully extracted from their fireside chairs and led out ('She's just coming...') into an icy hall to croak a greeting to the grandchildren ('Is that my sweet little Penelope?'). At three-minute intervals, a mechanical bleeping sound warned of the passing of time and of the expense. This useful reminder has now been silently removed by the Post Office in what some might consider a deceitful manner.

Here at 'Myrtlebank' we make rather a thing of the festive season. The hedges contain holly trees and the holly trees contain berries, and sprigs and twigs find their way indoors and are propped on pictures and stuck into puddings. The motherly ewes in the orchard are bulging significantly and with luck there will be lambs frisking on Christmas Day. Miss Entwhistle's front door is already (I write in earlyish December) decorated with a tasteful arrangement of holly, ribbons and brightly coloured glass balls. During the drought, our birds disappeared completely (just as well that this column wasn't a weekly ornithological article entitled 'Guests At My Tit Table') but now they are back again and I am treating them in the cold weather to liberal supplies of an all-purpose bird food called 'Swoop'. There is, of course, a robin. If I am late rising, this sagacious bird appears at my bedroom window looking reproachful and clearly saying 'Where on earth is our Swoop?'. Hard to credit, possibly, but there would be no point in reporting it if untrue. My Cousin Madge has a sweet tooth and so a cherrywood occasional stands ready, laden with soft centres, for her next visit. What we call 'chrysanths' are everywhere. Any moment now our social activities will be crowned by an invitation to hot punch and hostess dainties *chez* the Bultitudes. We are all set.

The most cheering local news concerns our highly agreeable and intelligent Rector, hard-working, underpaid, war-damaged and far from robust and awaiting an operation, who, after a number of troubled years, has happily married, for the second time. But alas, this silver lining has an episcopal cloud to go with it in the shape of Eric, our Bishop. His predecessor, the late Robert, our Bishop, author of 'Christian Ethics', was a somewhat austere figure who emanated from one of the dustier Oxford colleges (*'C'est magnifique mais ce n'est pas la gare'*) and once allowed himself to be coerced into blessing, in full canonicals, a new Exeter multi-chain-super-store, or whatever they are now called, where our Westward TV picked him up in the grocery section, calling down God's benison upon row after row of Heinz Baked Beans. I rather doubt whether Christianity figures very freely in the balance sheets of such emporia. It seems that austerity did not cease with the departure of Robert, our Bishop. Operating from plushy quarters in the Close, Eric, our Bishop, has been reported in the national press as expressing disapproval of our Rector's marital move. A Bishop is, like the rest of us, entitled to his views, strict ones apparently, and anyhow experience has long since forced one to abandon the naive and probably rather childish expectation that professional Christians will be a bit kinder, more generous in spirit and less beastly than the rest of us. History's pages are full of fairly rum bishops, both arch and plain. Some centuries ago there was a Bishop of Winchester who provided a useful facility in the M.3 area (a chain of brothels, chock-a-block with virile visitors). Bishops, who have usually had, if nothing else, brains, have found little difficulty in squaring awkwardnesses with their consciences. One wonders what actually goes through their heads as, dressed up like Christmas trees, they intone 'Blessed are the meek'. It is a church niche that has always appealed especially to retired headmasters, out on a limb and wondering where next to make nuisances of themselves. The assumption of the dog collar is followed by a token two years in a not too slummy parish, and then comes that unfailing promotion from the ranks into Glory. Rough luck on parish priests over whose heads these meteorites have shot and who have been at it, so to speak, all their working lives. Are there statistics to hand as to how many clerics have modestly refused promotion to bishop status and thereby made sure of inheriting the kingdom of heaven? Precious few, I bet.

Invited recently to appear (a return visit, I boastfully announce) on Thames Television and have a half-hour chat with the clever and delightful Mavis Nicholson, we fell to talking about religion. The ambiance of Thames Television is all that is most calming—a relaxed atmosphere, charming producers, and a studio staff that smiles whenever it is remotely possible to do so. This encourages confidences. Did I, Mrs Nicholson asked, believe in God? My view of God is a simple one, namely that if he exists at all he must be an outstandingly disagreeable old gentleman. This I duly trotted out, together with a suggested name for his habitation, 'Up-alofto'. Did I pray, then asked Mrs Nicholson, she herself revealing that her prayers used to be that she would become spiritually better and a worthier character. I then had to confess that until I gave up prayer in 1921 my prayers had usually been, as a keen model railwayman, that somebody would unexpectedly give me several yards more track. Nobody ever did and therefore, so depressingly meagre were the results of prayer, I prayed no more. Viewers in large numbers (it was an afternoon programme and so why weren't they doing something more useful?) reached for their pens and an avalanche of tracts, texts, printed prayers and booklets, together with letters, descended on me and is still descending. All polite, strange to say, save one, a crosspatch female believer in a residential hotel ('Go and boil your silly head!'). All written more in sorrow than in anger, with 'poor old you' the general theme. Some of the letters had over twenty biblical references. No letter was shorter than four pages. I answered them all, thinking it impolite not to do so. All the letters assured me repeatedly of the existence and kindly nature of the supreme being, but as I read them, I was struck by the fact that the writers seemed somehow to lack confidence. They protested too much and one seemed to sense behind it all a feeling of insecurity and almost of desperation. Could it be that it was themselves they were trying to persuade as much as poor old unbelieving me?

Disbelief in God doesn't deny one the solid comfort and reassurance obtainable from belief in an earthbound Christ and our midnight mass at Appleton is a pleasurable Christmas feature, though when the carols start I have to absent the mind, so painfully do they stir up the past and memories of the dead and gone and of times when the future seemed brighter than now. It was the carols that were, of course, partly the undoing of the admirable Mr. Heath. The electorate got muddled. It had become accustomed to seeing a spray-soaked figure in sou'-wester and jaunty yachting cap and of fixing this breezy chap in their minds as our sailor prime minister (echoes of George V who was always happily known as 'Our Sailor King', and all the world, as we know, loves a sailor). And then suddenly there he was, surpliced and waving a baton as Christians awoke and saluted the happy morn. Then the newspapers showed pictures of a vast grand piano being trundled into No. 10 and the muddle was complete. And then there was that voice that to an English ear was so difficult to 'place' (such a shame that that boat had to be called *Morning Cloud* when there were other Mornings available. Morning Glory, for instance. I do not include Morning Sickness).

I *say*, we've been together now for a year! Thank you for bearing with me. Happy Christmas.

CRITIC'S CORNER

FRONTAL ATTACK

The Glory of the Perfumed Garden. By Sir Richard Burton (Neville Spearman, 1975).

We all know what happened to the original English version of *The Perfumed Garden*, lovingly translated from the French in 1888 by Sir Richard Burton (and a snap exists of him assiduously at work). This rich panorama of Arabic sexual practice, from the lively quill of Shaykh Nafzawi and dating from 1410, was expanded down the years by the many authors who had additional happy thoughts on the subject. On Sir Richard's death, his manuscript was pounced on by Lady Burton who, scandalised by the many saucy portions, instantly popped them on the nearest bonfire, ensuring for herself both a lifetime and a posterity of violent condemnation.

But courage! Sir Richard's work lives again, now entitled *The Glory of the Perfumed Garden* (Neville Spearman. £3.75) and furnished by a 'professional translator', coyly anonymous though possibly American (there is a reference, as well there might be, to 'petting').

Those who do not obtain access to this particular Garden can hardly complain that their sexual education needs these days to hang fire. Illustrated information is everywhere to hand. *Playgirl*, the counterpart of *Playboy* and apparently destined for ladies who enjoy having a dekko at chaps in free-and-easy postures, is now even on sale in Harrods.

The Shaykh's book, though describing sexual deviations in some detail, opts pretty strongly for the straight stuff. Readers may care to know that sexual union is the very thing to cure headaches, mental disorder, clouded vision and sensations of suffocation. On the other hand, look out for involuntary twitchings, pain in the joints and itching. And for heaven's sake watch your diet:

Coitus after fish results in insanity, after milk in paralysis, after camel-meat and lentils in varicose veins and gout, after aubergines in hot flushes.

It's all a question of timing and checking with the cook. And for pity's sake, no activity before breakfast.

The author provides, in addition to various recommended gymnastics, a feast of assorted information:

—— There's nothing new about water-beds. Years ago, the Caliph Mutawakkil invented a large tank filled with mercury and covered with blankets 'which put him through the motions without his having to use any great effort'.

—— Marital consummation during the daytime *need not* be accompanied by a torchlight procession, but nicer with it, of course.

—— Weddings and funerals were often women's only chance of leaving the house at all and so cemeteries were frequently the scene of vigorous sexual activity.

—— 'Some procuresses carry rosaries and wear woollen clothing', which may remind NS readers of a winning entry in the competition about Misleading Advice for Foreigners ('There is no State-controlled harlotry but it may safely be assumed that any woman found *seated* in the National Portrait Gallery is a procuress').

—— If the loved one plays hard-to-get, a gift of pigeons is always popular.

—— The Queen of Sheba had hairy legs.

What, one wonders, will be the book's effect on the general public? Let us imagine a retired couple, Standish and Mildred Bulstrode, living quietly near Bognor. Major Bulstrode was, as they say, in teak and both have green fingers. They spot the book in Hoggit and Bumfield's window and snap it up, the words 'glory', 'garden' and 'perfume' persuading them that it is the last word on tobacco plant and night-scented stock.

Excitedly they read it through from cover to cover and instantly their lives are transformed. Mildred starts thinking of her breasts as ripe pomegranates, anoints them, as instructed, with the liquid from onions boiled in jasmine oil, and orders a camel from Gamages. At the golf club everybody remarks on Standish's new brightness of eye and vitality (he is no longer the listless competitor who makes such a poor showing in the

Monthly Medal). To the polite question 'How's the Missus, Bulstrode?' he now replies, 'She is as fair as the crescent moon and as slender as a deodar,' adding for good measure, 'Inkpens without ink avail a man little. No collops roast without skewers, nor can sails rise without a mast.' Then, with a glad cry of 'Now, home to my gazelle!' he dashes out, leaps into the Datsun and drives off, leaving a perplexed gathering round the bar. 'Poor old Bulstrode has gone right off his rocker.' They can hardly know that the Major is now very much *on* his rocker.

But only in moderation. As he himself so often says, 'Happy is he who has a box of dates from which he eats but once a day'. However, to make sure that the dates are available, Mildred revises her menus completely. For dinner she takes equal amounts of wild garlic, rocket seeds and Chinese ginger, mixing all to a paste in sesame oil. For starters there are celery seeds tossed in fat. Meanwhile Standish besieges Boots' for fresh supplies of bezoar (a stony deposit found in llamas' stomachs and, grated into drinks, splendid for helping things along).

Dining with the Bulstrodes at 'Gay Baskets' is something of a hazard. Startled guests find themselves sitting down to Indian millet, glasses of ewe's milk, nettles, manna, weaned camel's rennet, and a strange blackish substance. 'Whatever's this, Mildred?' 'Oh that. It's minced hyena's pizzle. I managed to get the very last one in Lethbridge's.'

Anxious to change the subject, somebody enquires about the fruit of the Bulstrodes' loins, a rather lumpy girl of thirty-three now working in the local kennels. 'What's the news of Mona?' The question is a sitter for the Major. 'A pearl from the treasures of the sea is a virgin untouched by the jeweller's drill.' When dining alone, the Bulstrodes tend to favour a somewhat gaseous diet but alas, the slightest instance of wind is a Ritual Impurity and must be immediately rectified by a Lesser Ablution (if the water's been cut off, make do with fine sand). The Bulstrodes, partial to baked beans, are for ever on the move.

And so to bed, after the Bognor muezzin has called them to prayer, with the Major feasting his eyes on Mildred, fragrant with amber, civet and musk and *troublante* as ever behind her yashmak, with her face 'as comely as the moon at full and eyes as lustrous as the antelope's'. And there is, in addition, the good book's comforting assertion that 'Women are like beds—the bulkiest are the softest.'

STRAWBERRIES AND CREAM

The Dukes. By Brian Masters (Blond & Briggs, 1975).

I am now happily in a position to help anybody anxious to mug up a novel subject and then cut a dash on *Mastermind*, the TV High IQ Quiz Programme. The subject is non-royal Dukes, but first a little of the somewhat thin information available from the Dukes themselves.

They have in general been far too occupied signing building contracts to put their pens to more literary uses, though the 8th Duke of Argyll did spread himself over 1,000 autobiographical pages. He provided, too, mind-tingling page headings —Crows and their Habits, Gladstone's Views on Russia, Visit to Leamington, Building a Lighthouse, Diseases of the Potato, Fossil Leaves in Mull, Table-turning in Albany (Bishop Wilberforce was caught cheating).

Inspired by this forebear, the 9th Duke of Argyll edited some eighteenth-century correspondence ('Letters, grave or gay, have always a freshness about them'), unearthed some mysterious domestic accounts ('To Coloured Pigg, 1/6. To a Dutch Crutch, 2/9'), and furnished joyous shouts from the moors at bang-bang time ('The Hills swarm with Roebucks and black Cocks') and helpful advice on gambling and boozing ('The best remedy is marriage').

There were also Jokes—a muddled butler proffering a dish with the words 'Grace, your Grouse?' and a sleepy Dean mishearing an offer of Benedictine as Benedictus Benedicat and providing a fervent 'Amen'.

Then there was the 1st Duchess of Newcastle who relates that her husband urged her to pawn her clothes in exchange for something for dinner, a different way of life from that of the 8th Duke of Devonshire and his comfortable Victorian existence

('In autumn well-to-do Englishmen, tranquillised by rural pursuits, reassemble in town').

But now to *Mastermind* and a dummy run. The lights lower, the Questioner picks up his sheaf of teasers and moistens the lips. We are off!
Q. What is your name?
A. Arthur Marshall.
Q. What is your profession?
A. I am an Old Age Pensioner and my subject is non-royal Dukes.
Q. How many are there?
A. There were 26 at the last count, all of them related to each other in one way or another. There have been several more but as a body they have been regularly pruned by beheadings for high treason. In cases where the victim was publicly hanged, the body was divided up and consolatory portions were distributed to neighbouring towns who had missed the main treat. This practice has now been given up.
Q. How do you recognise Dukes?
A. Nowadays they look much like anybody else but on solemn occasions you can easily pick them out for they wear coronets sporting eight gold strawberry leaves and the Queen addresses them as 'right trusty and entirely beloved cousins'.
Q. Does she always mean it?
A. Your guess is as good as mine.
Q. Tradition has held them to be, in general, boring. Is this so?
A. Far from it. They have been bizarre, intransigent, selfish, eccentric, hugely self-confident and with strong streaks of both delinquency and lunacy in their veins.
Q. Which has been the dottiest?
A. In a very strong field, pride of place must go to the 5th Duke of Portland who had a bulbous nose supporting two large warts, secured his trouser legs with string, hid behind an opened umbrella when stared at, wore a heavy sable coat in summer and had a choice of eighty-six wigs. He converted Welbeck Abbey in such a way that most of the rooms, including a ballroom capable of holding 2,000, were underground and required fifteen miles of tunnel.
Q. And the runner-up?
A. Difficult to say. The 12th Duke of St. Albans, a relatively recent figure, was delightfully unusual; he interrupted preachers

with shouts of 'Rubbish!', arrived for visits with his pyjamas in a brown paper bag, hoped to appear at the 1953 Coronation accompanied by a live falcon, and refused to be moved from a hotel which had caught fire and was burning merrily: 'Nonsense! Bring me some more toast.' And no fiddle-faddle after death either: 'Bury me where I drop.'

Q. Whence cometh your encyclopaedic knowledge?

A. It cometh partly from my own skilled researches but mainly from the splendidly painstaking and enormously readable and unstuffy endeavours of Brian Masters in his book.

Q. Would you say that on the whole Dukes have been a Good Thing or a Bad Thing?

A. A Good Thing. Most of them have had admirable taste in the matter of houses—Boughton, Woburn, Chatsworth, Goodwood. They have assembled superb collections of pictures, porcelain and so on, treasures which they now, for a modest fee, share with us. They have an excellent record as humane employers. Some of them have been perhaps a little mean: the 1st Duke of Marlborough refused to dot his i's in order to save ink, but they have undoubtedly done more good than harm.

Q. Are we likely to see any new dukedoms?

A. Improbable. No monarch since Victoria has created one, though a dukedom was allegedly offered to Churchill. Previously it was quite a pastime, Charles II, a grateful king, creating over twenty, among them five of his nephews and six bastard sons. At least thirteen Prime Ministers can trace their ancestry back to the lusty union between that supremely charming sovereign and Barbara Villiers, a restless lady who subsequently notched up ten other lovers, her interests ranging widely from Wycherley to a performer on the tightrope.

Q. What else have you to tell us?

A. Oh goodness, there's just so *much*! The 4th Duke of Queensberry bathed in milk and was bored by the Thames: 'There it goes, flow, flow, flow.' The Buccleugh possessions are greater than any private land-owner in either Britain or Europe. The late Duke of Norfolk had a no-nonsense approach to lady dinner guests: 'I have only two topics of conversation—cricket and drains. Choose.' There has been one Double Duchess—Louise who, on the death of Manchester, switched to Devonshire. The Duke of Devonshire owns no land in Devonshire but manages quite well in Derbyshire. For a time the 7th Duke of Leinster ran a tea-shop in Rye. Casanova visited the 2nd Duke of Northumberland at Alnwick and apparently passed on to him some of his left-overs.

Q. Er, thank you. Now, do you recall that some years ago while Miss Hermione Gingold was giving of her remarkable best at a matinée, a child in the front row said loudly, 'Mummy, what is that woman *for*?'
A. I do so recall.
Q. What, then, are Dukes *for*?
A. Pass.

STILL A PEASANT AT HEART

Nicole Nobody. By The Duchess of Bedford (W. H. Allen, 1974). £3.50.

'I hate being photographed. I always look like a mashed potato.'

The Duchess of Bedford brings a jolly, carefree freshness to a literature not overburdened with ducal memoirs and, being French, has a firmly practical approach to life—and death ('Harrods will come and collect me pronto. I want my body stuffed with herbs').

In youth, when she 'was always up to some mischief', the *jolie* mashed potato did not lack admirers ('Would you like to come under my umbrella?'). There was even a wonky Marquess who enjoyed barking like a dog under tables and being chained to chairs ('You should be ashamed of yourself').

A humdrum 'arranged' marriage produced four handsome children and assorted shocks, including saucy *cartes postales* ('At first glance I thought the subjects might be acrobats').

The war years were spent courageously in Paris, bicycling along with machine-gun parts in her saddle-bag, passing on verbal code messages ('I have the nail of my grandmother'), and discouraging amatory German advances ('I spat out the word "swine"'). And in victory, conquering Texans misbehaved and had to be fought off ('I was revived with Calvados').

Then, after some domestic upsets ('*Tante* Emilie had dropped her wig in the lavatory pan'), a brief encounter in a Manchester hotel ('He was a superb lover') prudently followed by a course in Judo ('I simply threw him over my shoulders'), a spell as a television producer, and divorce in 1956, it was on to Woburn and the 13th Duke ('I felt cherished, wanted, needed. I blossomed').

Those planning to throw open their houses will find in *Nicole Nobody* plenty to put them off. 'Woburn has been a devouring duty,' with its 120 rooms, 97 telephones, 565 windows, 13 miles of walls, and various tourist attractions ('Each year we set aside £10,000 for renovating or building new loos').

And you never know what eccentric visitors may not get up to, even with a Duke.:

> Ian was as white as a sheet and I asked what was the matter. He had encountered a mad woman. She had entered the kiosk where he was selling souvenirs, put a vice-like arm around him, and with the other arm had tried to undo his trousers.

Still, there was a fine mixed grill of friends—Paul Getty, 'Boofy' Arran, George Brown during his ebullient Foreign Secretary period and with, it appears, a kiss 'like a vacuum-cleaner', and our very own Barbara Cartland:

> With a *décolletage* that plunged like a great white glacier, and absolutely dripping with diamonds, she stepped out of a white Rolls-Royce. A large necklace hung from her throat down to her great quivering bosom... Barbara was at her best, incredible and marvellous.

And then there was the excitement at Woburn of the Miss World Competition, with Gulbenkian complaining about his dinner partner ('Nicole, I am not very keen on my Miss Turkey') and Bob Boothby, in expansive mood, trying to coax a belly dance out of Miss Egypt ('Of course she obliged').

The Duchess has sailed through it all splendidly ('I can wear a tiara with aplomb') because, you see, underneath it all, the glitter and the glamour, 'I have perhaps to this day remained a peasant girl at heart.' *Tiens!*

YOURS TRULY

The First Cuckoo. By Kenneth Gregory (Allen & Unwin, 1976).

Nowadays I frequently hear talk on the wireless about what is evidently a current matter of concern but which, as so often with technical subjects, is incomprehensible to me. I refer to people complaining about the erosion of their differentials. Now what on earth can these be? Do I, as a *New Statesman* writer, have differentials? If so, are they being eroded? If they are, who is being so beastly as to erode them? What should I do to preserve my differentials? To whom should I write? Would an anxious letter from me ever get printed in these very pages?

Well, it might. Those that write letters to the *New Statesman* are, and very properly, on the whole a serious-minded body. Helpfully they provide comments on and solutions to many of life's complexities—abortion, Mr. Heath, dockland, Papal pronouncements on sex, uppish adolescents, Lord Ryder, noise levels, immigration, students, Solzhenitsyn, and other agitating matters that now bring one nervous twitches in their wake.

But, if turned down here, would my worries ever get an airing in, say, *The Times*? Doubtful. Too serious a subject, probably. At just about this period of the year (I write in mid-April) all *Times* readers are everywhere on the alert for the first cuckoo. What is the earliest record of a hearing? Who can ever forget the excitement on February 6th, 1913, when, long before sumer was icumen in, lhude sang cuckoo to a Mr. Lydekker and his under-gardener in the heart of leafy Hertfordshire. They hastened, naturally, to inform *The Times*, but had later to confess that their ears had deceived them and the gladsome sound turned out to have come from a bricklayer melodiously at work nearby.

We owe this useful information to *The First Cuckoo*, a wholly fascinating selection, by Kenneth Gregory, from letters to *The*

Times between 1900 and 1975. The immediate impression one gets from a first reading is of a delightful frivolity. The idea that all such letters emanated from Pall Mall and were penned, in mounting fury, by choleric old colonels, is plainly a myth.

The correspondents here gathered together (and not an Archbishop, Lord Chief Justice, Director-General of the BBC or Warden of All Souls among them) are from a wide range of professions, social statuses and bank balances. Top People may Take *The Times* but they are by no means the only ones. Fortunately, the great crises of the century, about which we already know too depressingly much, are only mentioned *en passant*, preference being given to wit and invective, innocence and nostalgia. 'The sole criterion for inclusion has been a letter's readability' assures Mr. Gregory. We are in good hands.

Writers have considered almost any facts of value. Those of us who have been wondering, and for years now, who could possibly have been the very first Bishop to wear spectacles need wonder no more, for here is the answer. It was, clearly, Walter de Stapledon (he was lynched by the mob in Exeter in 1326, his specs being subsequently valued at the considerable sum of 2s). And the first horse to enjoy assisted eyesight? Why, that was a Manchester gelding in 1888, the oculist prescribing concave spectacles for its weak eyes. The horse, with the gig-lamps fitted securely on, 'shewed signs of the keenest pleasure'. If put out to pasture without his spectacles, he would hang moodily and myopically about, whinnying in a plaintive minor key.

There is no end to the astonishments. How extraordinary to find John Masefield displaying a quite unexpected and detailed knowledge of the white slave trade, its evil tentacles reaching as far afield as Shepton Mallet and Stoke Poges. He writes, much concerned, about 'good-looking housemaids' being enticed to the capital, there getting snapped up at £50 a go and whisked off to the continent in a tall ship with a star to steer them by: and thence, by easy stages, to Buenos Aires, then rated the peak place for gentlemen requiring free-and-easy female companionship.

Every day esoteric information of the most varied kind is unselfishly passed on. The leader (Imam) of the Mosque at Woking lets it be known that the Mosque neither stocks nor sells Turkish Delight (please apply elsewhere). Side-saddle is the *only* way for expectant mothers. To put paid to mosquitos, sprinkle your bed with grated myrrh. If poor children were to walk shoeless to school it would beneficially harden their feet and prevent colds. Conan Doyle played for the MCC and once dismissed W. G. Grace with the loftiest donkey-drop ever seen at Lord's. Hitler was not a corporal but a lance-corporal. Grey squirrels can make quite a tasty casserole ('make' in the sense of 'form the main ingredient of': cf, 'he made the evening').

Sometimes a subject sets off a chain reaction. A claim from Sussex to be the county with the most curious surnames (Pitchfork, Slybody, Stillborne, Fidge, Padge and Beatup) instantly brings showers of weird names from all over, including those of villages (Helions Bumpstead, Mucking, Plush and Shellow Bowells, which only just avoids sounding like something else).

In due course, the famous and eminent pop up. Bernard Shaw complains that at Covent Garden he found himself behind a lady with half a dead bird pinned decoratively over her right ear, adding that if he had turned up at the doors with a dead grouse on top of his head he would have been refused admission. Millicent, Duchess of Sutherland speaks out for allowing policemen to chew chewing-gum ('It has a steadying effect on their nerves. I encourage my chauffeur to chew'). P. G. Wodehouse supplied the answer to the burning question as to just how far Bertie Wooster's chin receded. Lady Edward Cecil, bewailing, and as early as 1910, the inefficiency of our railways, was outraged at being charged excess for her and her maid's hand luggage ('One has learned to expect anything from the South-Eastern Railway Company'). And in 1933, and in the same month that Hitler became Chancellor of Germany, the lynx-eyed and wide-awake Neville Chamberlain wrote to say that he had spotted a grey wagtail in St. James's Park.

Particularly recommendable are the choices from the war years, both the Kaiser's and Hitler's. Should children wear gasmasks when blackberrying? Were dachshunds being cruelly treated because of their German connection? If meat is in short supply, why ever don't people switch to grouse? One wonders again, and for the umpteenth time, how on earth we muddled through.

YUM YUM

Consuming Passions. By Philippa Pullar (Hamish Hamilton, 1971).

Mrs. Pullar's book announces itself as being a history of English food and appetite but in fact it is much more—a highly digestible potted survey of social life and behaviour from the Roman occupation onwards, though she finds time too to hark back to Celtic cannibalism (the palms of the hands are, *on dit*, especially succulent: serve with a tossed salad).

She harks back to much else besides and casts her net wide. The humble medlar was originally known as 'open-aerse'. In 1659 Walter Rumsey invented an ingenious stomach-brush with which the anxious could healthfully scour within. The founder of Caius College, Cambridge, existed during the last years of his life only upon human milk. Bleeding takes care of almost any ailment, putting paid to gout, haemorrhoids and acne, but when feeling an acute attack of ague coming on, instantly apply hot pickled herrings to the feet.

'Appetite' includes sexual hunger (our authoress excels at hilarious indecent jokes). While gluttonous Dr. Johnson was summoning back the lobster sauce in order to pour it over his plum pudding, other bodily needs were being attended to in the nearby Covent Garden area. Special virgins were prepared for customers with defloration mania. Mrs. Whackum and Miss Birch were available and whips rose and fell. For deft manual attentions (at two gns a go) there were Polly Nimble-wrist from Oxford and Jenny Speedyhand from Mayfair, while a select establishment for lonely ladies requiring the attentions of muscled rustics was tastefully run by Mary Wilson.

Fascinating facts abound. There is a description of a medieval feast that is as rich and vivid as a Balzac *conte drolatique*. In the 13th century, archdeacons held drinking competitions and the

Bishop of Winchester had an interesting lay side-line (18 brothels, jammed to the doors). You could get three roast thrushes for 2d, while a dunghill mallard set you back 3½d. A master cook could earn a salary equivalent to £3,000. *Blamangers* were a meat mousse, subsequently demoted to a pallidly wobbling breast-like substance called 'shape'. Most recipes had a Beetonesque lavishness (Sir Walter Raleigh's Sack Posset required a quart of boiling cream). The Pepyses' basement latrine was insufficiently fragrant (wise guests held on till they got home) and the finest thing in the world for discouraging untimely Elizabethan erections was nettles in the codpiece. To enliven that stodgy dinner-party for the firm's senior partners, why not copy the revered Emperor Augustus, who liked to remove his friends' wives between courses, returning flushed and in disarray ('Another kidney, anybody?').

The first fish-and-chippery arrived in 1902 and from then on the rot set in—Tango Teas, the appallingly lean Thirties ('The Survival of the Fattest'), Woolton pie in a hay-box, deep-frozen goodies for all seasons, mouth-watering Juicyburgers, cholesterol, obesity, and a final ungainly exit from this vale of tears via a really massive thrombosis.

Does Mrs. Pullar, in her understandable excitement over her treasure-trove, occasionally over-write? Does she put too much faith in that mendacious gas-bag, Frank Harris? Possibly. But this is a piffling price to pay for a book so readable and so engagingly full of unstuffy knowledge, wisdom and just straight fun.

FORGING A CAREER

This Solemn Mockery. By John Whitehead (Arlington, 1973).

Imitation may be the sincerest form of flattery, and, in the field of forgery, if it is well done then by golly it can be profitable.

The most popular paper forgeries have been, naturally, those delightful high-denomination bank-notes. While producing some of the best Vermeers ever painted, Van Meegeren made, and rightly, a fortune. And the famous and plausible Thomas J. Wise had, 60 or so years ago, a vastly valuable line in his very own first editions of Keats, Shelley and others.

John Whitehead's *This Solemn Mockery*, an excellent survey of some of these gifted confidence tricksters, concentrates on the art of literary forgers. What odd names they tended to have—De Gibler-Byron, Psalmanazar, Denis Vrain-Lucas, and loyal old Wenceslaus Hanka who, fretting in 1817 about the absence of literature in his beloved Bohemia, effortlessly ran up some centuries of poems to bolster its sagging prestige.

In the 18th century the Immortal Bard, with the assistance of William Ireland, provided a new play called 'Vortigern and Rowena' (just the one, all-star performance at Drury Lane) and, disregarding the boos, Ireland pressed boldly on with a letter from Elizabeth I to Shakespeare:

> Wee didde receive your prettye verses good Masterre William through the hands of our Lord Chamberlyne and wee do complemente thee onne thyre great excellence.

Whatte could be fayrer than thatte?

By 1800 autographs were valuable collector's items, and Sotheby's did a brisk trade. Vrain-Lucas, a Frenchman, muscled in on this industry and produced letters from Galileo to Pascal, from Rabelais, Pliny, Mary Magdalene ('Yesterday was *quite* a day!'), Shakespeare, Cleopatra (planning to educate her son in healthful Marseilles) and the Venerable Bede, all of whom wrote in modern French and on nice clean paper. This particular rot had set in in the fourth century when Eusebius, in his history of Christianity, accepted as genuine a letter from Christ to Agbar, King of Edessa ('Greetings, my good Agbar').

Such was the market for the *vrai* Vrain-Lucas wares that to satisfy the eager and gullible customers he had to produce an average of eight new pieces every day for eight years—a staggering output.

Those planning a career in forgery may care to know the sentence passed on Vrain-Lucas when his deceptions were discovered—two years' jug and a fine of a mere £25, a flea-bite when compared with his handsome profit of over £6,000. Out, then, with those plates and start scratching.

BEATIE IN THE BOIS

The Strenuous Years: Diaries, 1948–55. By Cecil Beaton (Weidenfeld & Nicolson, 1973).

'When Emerald Cunard took notice of me, I felt I had not lived in vain.' Well, there we are then. Each to his target. Sir Cecil Beaton is nothing if not honest and 'no snob welcomes another who has risen with him' puts paid to Evelyn Waugh (a less agreeable diarist).

The Strenuous Years is very much the weird mixture as before, with 'Beatie boy' (Garbo's name for him) still enamoured of his mashed Swede, buying her woollen combinations from Harrods, joining her in Paris ('Off we whizzed to the Bois'), and then seeing her with Another ('I felt slightly rattled').

A row with the Oliviers ('Phew!') and a trip to New York and its 'electric ozone' are followed by Coronation photographs of Royalty ('They confessed their feet hurt') and anxiety as to whether the Queen Mother had sufficient servants:

> I realise I am exaggerating when I write the following but there is more than an element of truth when I say that I did not realise how life can be ruthless, even to queens.

Back and forth we smartly shuttle—the Duff Coopers at Chantilly, the Lunts in New York, Audrey Hepburn in South Audley Street ('I felt that she cut through to a basic understanding').

And there is a splendid story about a Lady Bingham (her appearance 'verged on wit') who was compelled by a madman to undress in a railway carriage and climb into the luggage rack, where he feasted his eyes on her charms until alighting at Vauxhall.

Sir Cecil is as bravely individual in prose as in life and his diaries (revised? altered? cut? and if not, why not?) often read as though a second-rate translator, dictionary in hand, has been at work on some foreign tongue. He talks with his country-based mother ('I try to impart the news of my busy urban days'). He visits 'the venerable master of *belles lettres*', Max Beerbohm ('We were busy imbibing every nuance').

Being made to talk with unacceptable people is 'being forced vis-à-vis'. There is a Downing Street party ('people displayed their nicest moods') and Lady Churchill ('There is still fire and dash in the consort of the old warrior'—which reads like an O Level Latin sentence).

On this showing, the written word is really not for Sir Cecil, yearn as he may to be a writer. He is altogether too carefree about what may be allowed to appear in print. Highly gifted cobblers must stick to their lasts, or, as our subject might phrase it, must adhere to their selected methods of livelihood.

IS MY SCREW LOOSE?

Handbook of Lawn Mower Repair. By Franklynn Peterson (John Murray, 1974).

Spring at last, with the suburbs echoing joyously to the cosy whirr of the motor-mower, sweetly tuned and richly lubricated and all set for the demands of the peak cutting season.

At 'The Laurels' they've checked their oil viscosity, adjusted their nozzle valves, tested their flywheels and, finding all in applepie order, Mr. Hopcroft has gamely opened full throttle on the croquet lawn.

At 'The Elms' they have ejected all foreign matter trapped inside their cylinder heads and, supremely confident in their exhaust mufflers and nipples, have now wisely crowded on more power for that rough piece of grass by the barbecue.

At 'Gay Baskets' the Hendersons have washed their Dry Element Air Cleaner in a non-sudsing detergent and, proud possessors of a brand new Two Piece Maxiflo gravity carburettor, they're chugging along in fine style by the herbaceous.

Only 'Dun Roamin' is silent with Major Beamish peering anxiously into the vitals of his sullen, lifeless machine. What are those beads of encrusted carbon? Are his bolts loose or his parts worn? And he and 'Birdie' Beamish had been planning a refreshing round of clock golf....

If only he had invested in the *Handbook of Lawn Mower Repair*, his blades would now be whirling over the green turf with the rest of them. The book's author, knowledgeable Franklynn Peterson, is as aware as anybody of the slightly comical side of his subject and the esoteric nature of his information ('If some of the terms are unfamiliar, don't despair') and is all encouragement to the tyro:

> The mysterious, greasy noisy world beneath that painted cover on your lawn mower engine need not intimidate you....

Taking wrench in hand, expose that mysterious world down under.

Now, let's just see. Before I myself cut a generous swathe, is everything as it should be? What of my clutch assembly? Have I sufficient tappet clearance? Is my throttle shaft and bushing wobbly? Have I added an extra gasket to my sump? Are there readily to hand my feeler gauge and my vice-grip pliers? Yes, yes, and so off I purr, making mowing history with my 109 cc., two-stroke Trimalong.

In a diagram entitled 'Exploded View of Parts in a Well-Built Hand-Powered Mower' the excitement mounts, with thrilling talk of Bottom Handle Sections and Ball Cups, of Jackshafts and Retaining Rings. Then there are these huge . . . but I won't spoil it for you.

ROLL OUT THE BARREL

As I See It. By Paul Getty (W. H. Allen, 1976).

I much enjoy a really mind-boggling piece of statistical information. Was I told it, or did I read or dream it, that there is enough ground space for every human being alive today to be able to stand, if in rather restricted comfort, upon the Isle of Wight. Just imagine the queues for the Ventnor 'toilets' and the linguistic confusions in Woolworth's, while the Island itself gently subsides into the Solent. Then the Hoover dam in America, the telly informs me, holds back sufficient water for each individual in the world to have a 1,400 gallon share (if this is so, kindly send mine along immediately). The *Radio Times*, chock-a-block as ever with wholesome information, startles one by saying that a thimbleful of matter on a neutron star weighs 1,000 million tons. And I shyly put forward my own sad statistic which is that the number of sound decibels made by the chugging of summer traffic on the dreaded Exeter by-pass is rather fewer than the sum total of those caused by the loud thudding of solid British plimsolls sportingly losing ('Oh I say, good shot!') at Wimbledon.

    I had hoped, on approaching, somewhat gingerly, the late Paul Getty's illustrated autobiography, *As I See It*, about to be published by W. H. Allen at £6.00, to be dazzled with oil and petroleum statistics to use as dinner-table conversation-stoppers, and I was in no way disappointed. The book bulges with hard facts straight from the wellheads. Like his rich father before him, Getty had a sort of built-in oil-diviner. He could sense the delightful stuff squelching away deep down beneath his boots. It is, clearly, an electrifying moment when the drilling ceases and plop!, that first well starts gushing. And the fun could hardly be said to die down when it's the hundredth well. Who would not rejoice to find liquid money pouring out of a hole in the ground at the rate of 15,000 barrels a day?

Well, rejoicing is not perhaps the first activity one thinks of in this connection. That unhappy face, at almost all its stages, tells all.

> The life you lead sets all your nerves a-jangle,
> Your love affairs are in a hopeless tangle

sang the incomparable Delysia to an appropriately muted Hermione Baddeley in Cochran's revue, *On With The Dance*, and although Noël Coward's song was directed at a girl, the same conditions often apply to poor little rich guys. Hopeless tangle hardly describes Getty's marital forays. In fairly rapid succession, five hopeful ladies tip-toed to join him at the altar, smiling heroically and confident of only one thing. There would be enough house-keeping money. They probably sensed that the venture was doomed from the start. There's really nothing a lady can do, basically, if her charms don't measure up in attraction to a busy day at the well-head and more and more barrels of lovely oily oil. And charming indeed the girls were. There were, in order of collapse, Jeanette Demont ('vibrant and magnetic'), Allene Ashby ('she excelled as an equestrienne'), Adolphine Helmle ('she radiated vitality and vivacity'), Ann Rork ('a lovely brunette') and Louise Lynch ('a Society Chanteuse'). But alas, ride, sing, magnetise and vibrate how they may, they just couldn't lick those gushers. There were children, here and there, and it says much for the whole lot of them, and Getty himself, that they all managed to remain friends. And he adds something that has the ring of truth about it: 'Women tend to stick longer to failure than to success.'

But now to the main nub of the affair, the cash. 'My wealth is not a subject I relish discussing.' He does, however. By the age of 24, a dollar millionaire. By the age of 80, 'certainly above a billion dollars' with a Getty family trust of twice that amount. Even though an American billion is a mere 1,000 million, that's not pea-nuts.

The rich and famous tend to have as friends only the rich and famous, then nobody gets out of their depth and becomes tiresome, and the text is peppered throughout with names, some of which make one thoughtful. There are Aly Khan, Thyssen, and the Woolworth heiress Barbara Hutton (when she married Cary Grant, they were known as 'Cash and Cary'). There is, of course, Onassis (that yacht, the *Christina*, cost £180,000 a year to run).

The Duke of Windsor (it was, far from unacceptably, 'David' and 'Paul'), Randolph Churchill, Garbo, Lord Thomson and Youssoupoff all pop up. There was enormous entertaining at Sutton Place, once owned by Lord Northcliffe. There were additional houses all over the place, and a suite at the Ritz. And willing to take the rough with the smooth were numerous unknown females who wrote in out of the blue with friendly suggestions ('I am willing to marry you for $100,000 cash payable at the time of the wedding').

One can but admire his application and astuteness and there is something very agreeable about him. The longing to be liked (a condition not unknown in Americans), the love of small children, the generosity, the politeness, the ability to laugh at himself. He does not, unfortunately, write very well. The sentences lack zing and he is apt to sound off on unprofitable subjects—civil servants, crime, governments, taxes, sex, socialism, and the American postal service (it loses, I am astounded to learn, even more than our own once did). The fondness for England—he did two terms of PPE at Magdalen College, Oxford—and the snobbery are touching. His money has employed, and happily, thousands of people. The Getty art museum is there for all posterity to enjoy.

The secret of the success was due as much to personal supervision as to anything. When the Middle East was being opened up, he prudently mugged up Arabic in order to chat with King Saud and swiftly get down to brass tacks with *Wain zait, wain fluss?* ('Where is the oil? Where is the money?'). They soon found both (82,000 barrels daily). 'You know, Paul,' said Lord Beaverbrook, 'I've always felt that I had a reserved seat in life.' And the same thing goes, Mr. Getty implies, for himself, in which case it would be foolish to give it up and move back among the standees, bitter though it is to discover that happiness doesn't necessarily exist in the orchestra stalls.

'I am periodically subject to gloomy spells.' And with good reason. Understandably wary and suspicious, guarded by a security force and Alsatian dogs, a failed husband, he was cursed with the appalling urge to go on and on, work harder and harder, and acquire, quite needlessly, more and more. Perhaps the book should be re-titled *As I Seize It*. Strange that it should have been really rather unpleasant to have been the richest man in the world. Apart from, say, about £200,000, one envies him nothing.

BRAMAH RAMS & BATH BUNS

Paxton's Palace. By Anthony Bird (Cassell, 1976).

When the Crystal Palace was removed from its 1851 exhibition site in Hyde Park and reassembled on Sydenham Hill, Madame Clara Novello sang there and let out a high B-flat of such startling power that officials looked anxiously about them, fearing that the Meccano-like construction would collapse and shower them with glass.

They should have had more faith in Joseph Paxton. His building, designed for six months' use, stood for 85 years. This engineering genius had begun life as a gardener to the Duke of Devonshire, and his revolutionary design splendidly fulfilled Albert the Good's brainwave of a giant exhibition of all that was best in the world's art and industry ('All, *all* the work of my beloved angel,' cooed the angel's wife).

It was the inspiration of somebody on *Punch* to call the structure the Crystal Palace, and *Paxton's Palace* tells us fascinatingly how it was built. The facts astonish.

It required 900,000 square feet of sheet glass, and its enclosed area amounted to 33 million cubic feet (at a cost of a penny a foot). It was put up in 22 weeks and fitted out and painted in 16, in a tasteful *mélange* of white, red, Cambridge blue and a strongish yellow.

In 1851 alone the visitors managed between them to eat 943,691 Bath buns. The building was enormously profitable, the lavatories alone netting a cool £1,769 and setting a fashion: at that time, in the world's richest capital city, there was not a single public lavatory and the mind boggles as to how they all managed.

The non-engineering mind becomes bemused by the liberality of Mr. Bird's technical details. Were there *enough* sheerlegs? What of Bramah hydraulic rams and diagonal tie-bars? Is lateral stability fully dependent on internal portal bracing? How many saw-kerfs to a stake-pin? Would the condensation globules be small enough to slide down the glass and not go plop on agitated heads beneath?

They were and they didn't. All was triumph, despite the gloomy forecast of a Colonel Sibthorp that foreign riff-raff would flood the country, assassinate Victoria, introduce bubonic plague and idolatry and turn Kensington into a vast brothel. Paxton thought of everything, even S-shaped ventilators which put paid to 'museum foot' and the delighted Queen paid more than 40 visits ('My poor Albert is terribly fagged').

One more fact. The building, though seeming to be all graceful iron and glass, contained 600,000 cubic feet of timber, which explains why, when it went up in 1936, it went in a blaze of glory (89 fire engines), somewhat inconveniencing the Four Square gospellers who had planned to meet there for communal baptism in a heated tank.

MAVIS, ALIAS BUNGALOOSIE

Beautiful and Beloved: The Life of Mavis de Vere Cole. By Roderic Owen and Tristan de Vere Cole (Hutchinson, 1974).

Beautiful and beloved, certainly, but latterly really a bit of a bother, making an untidy end, haughty and incoherent, amid empty whisky bottles in S.W.1 and awash not only with alcohol but also self-pity.

She had come a long way. Born in 1908 as Mabel Wright, the daughter of a Charlton grocery assistant, she later blossomed in a St. Ives council house into startlingly attractive girlhood (in a happy snap at the age or 14 she is already *troublante* to a degree and with her 'canvas spread for love').

It wasn't long in coming. From scullery maid, she graduated to being a Wimbledon clergyman's children's governess. What she taught the child is far from clear, but she knew a trick or two to pass on to their Dad, these activities leading to the sack and a job amid Veeraswamy's savoury curries in Swallow Street. And on to the happy day when she caught hold of a gentleman's coat tails as he was whisking out of the Regent Palace and, swiftly enamoured, he married her.

He turned out to be the 47-year-old Etonian, Horace de Vere Cole (born, appropriately, in Blarney), known world-wide as the Prince of Practical Jokers and almost permanently rigged up as the Sultan of Zanzibar's uncle or The Anglican Bishop of Madras (one merry morning he visited a public school and, unasked, confirmed several boys).

But, alas, marriage to Mabel was no joke at all. Men seemed to come so naturally her way. Though she preferred them tall and thin, she had a long affair with Augustus John, with a Judge thrown in, and many others. She was in no way a professional entertainer: she just liked love.

'Mabel' became 'Mavis' and then 'Maris', and such a tasty morsel simply invited nicknames (to poor, speedily-bankrupt Horace she was either 'Bungaloosie' or 'Darling Woffles'). And then, clothes were a bother and she constantly peeled off ('My breasts love the Ouse, after a dip therein they are as hard as bullets') and then burst into verse:

> It was so dark
> I stood quite stark
> And let the breeze
> Tickle my kneeze.

She was nice and above all she was jolly and a great fascinator. The distinguished archaeologist, Mortimer Wheeler, married her, explaining his addiction by saying: 'You see some chocolates and you've got to eat them, even if you know you'll be sick afterwards.'

A son had appeared, whom she loved but did not allow to interfere with her busy social and amatory life ('She would park him in the Ladies' at the Berkeley'). The son and Roderic Owen have splendidly extracted the maximum fun from these goings-on and, in *Beautiful and Beloved*, they write admirably and tactfully about what is basically a tragedy.

The disastrous evening came when, doubtless 'a bit whoozy', she drew a bead on agreeable Lord Vivian and plugged him in the abdomen. The subsequent gaol sentence, though reasonably short, had a shattering effect on her which she fought, like many others, with the help of strong waters.

'Kindness is the keynote of your character,' wrote one admirer, adding: 'But you do get a bit ratty when tiddly.' Tiddly moments multiplied and eventually filled her life: 'With an angelic look on her face, down she'd slide to the floor—there to close her eyes or be sick.'

Not the prettiest of pictures. But she has brought great happiness to a number of lives. Her ashes are scattered in Cadogan Gardens. Spare her a kind thought as your bus rumbles nearby.

WHERE THE NUTS COME FROM

You're a brick, Angela! By Mary Cadogan and Patricia Craig (Gollancz, 1975).

'Life is really very quaint,' muses the feather-brained Lady Kitty in Maugham's *The Circle*. 'Sad too, of course, but oh *so* quaint. Often I lie in bed at night and have a good laugh to myself when I think just how quaint life is.' True indeed, and quaint also are the innumerable disconnected trivia with which one's own feather brain is cluttered. Why should one uselessly remember that Queen Mary whistled a lot (when alone), or that the German for a potato pancake is *Kartoffelpuffer*, or that Ethel Smyth was once engaged to Oscar Wilde's brother, or that the lovely Mabel St. John, prolific authoress of girls' school stories in the *Girls' Realm*, was in fact a man called Henry Cooper and was Gladys Cooper's brother.

In the 1930s when I was, via the BBC, inflicting on the listening public imitations of schoolmistresses—headmistresses giving an end-of-term speech, botany mistresses leading a nature ramble, etc.—I was conscientious and keen to get my scholastic facts right. This led to a close study of the matchless stories of Angela Brazil and also to what might be called Field Work, actual visits to girls' schools. It was simple enough to get gullible headmistresses to go into their routine by trumping up some imaginary god-daughter, a dear little scrap called Bumps now approaching school age and whose parents were abroad and had asked me to look about on their behalf. This behaviour, I now see, was both disgraceful and actionable but it brought rich results.

One school was particularly rewarding. Surrey. 120 boarders. Gravel soil (always a mysterious 'plus' in school prospectuses. Why? Purer water? Deeper drains? Less typhoid?). Church of England and a headmistress of whom the entire school was plainly terrified. This is as it should be. The prime function of a headmistress is to come unexpectedly round a corner and stumble on something discreditable.

Deep in chat, we went here, we went there. In the sick-room, a prostrate and white-faced patient, spotting Miss Winters (as I shall call her) and feeling that some sort of respectful gesture was required of her, suddenly sat bolt upright in bed, as cremated corpses are said to do in the initial stages. In the garden, we found, as I had hoped, two famished juniors entangled in the raspberry canes and desperately munching (order marks and impots galore).

We were walking along a passage, with Miss Winters waxing hot on the necessity for order and tidiness. 'A place for everything', she said, as though inventing it, 'and everything in its place.' Take macintoshes, for example. A special, large macintosh cupboard was an essential (we were evidently approaching it). Numbered pegs, each with its macintosh. Then one knew where one was. A hint of rain, a shouted command, a lightning dash to the cupboard, and there you were: every girl safely macintoshed. We stopped, and Miss Winters proudly flung open the cupboard door. Not a macintosh in sight. Not even any pegs to support them. But the cupboard was not empty. It contained a very large lawn-mower. Miss Winters was in no way defeated. 'Ah. Evidently some little administrative re-arrangement.' We swept on.

I was invited, and I can't think why, to stay for lunch. At Mademoiselle's French-speaking table the usual chat could be heard going on ('*Voulez-vous passer les verts*'). At the staff table we were a cowed little group. I longed to pour gin down their throats, and mine. Women are usually, as individuals, possessors of splendid senses of humour, but *en masse* humour tends to disappear. I attempted to lighten things. Pained looks, and serve me right.

In the afternoon, a lantern lecture, 'Our English Architectural Heritage', presented by a whiskery male nondescript and with Miss Bentley at the lantern's controls, ready to spring into action at the sound of the lecturer's clicker. The hall lights were extinguished and everything that could go wrong went wrong. Slides came in either in the wrong order or the wrong way up. By the time the latter were righted, the heat from the lamp had affected them and they started excitingly to boil and bubble and the colours ran. Miss Bentley, understandably overwrought, mistook almost any sound for a click. Four seconds of Chatsworth and away it shot, to be instantly replaced by Woburn: and that whizzed off before we had any time to drink in the splendours, and Hampton Court came juddering on upside down. Neither Miss Winters nor Whiskers himself seemed much to mind. Suddenly, a sharp cry from the apparatus. Poor Miss Bentley had singed herself.

I was reminded of the rather daunting atmosphere engendered on that gravel soil while reading Mary Cadogan and Patricia Craig's *You're a brick, Angela!*, an all-embracing survey of girls' fiction from 1839 to the present day. Here they all are—dear Miss Brazil herself, of course, the Susan Coolidge 'Katy' books, *Daddy-Long-Legs*, the Abbey School stories, Enid Blyton, and so on—all skilfully potted and ticketed. Messrs Gollancz, serious-minded and why not, have evidently requested their authoresses not to neglect the 'social implications' of the material under examination but all its jollity comes bursting through willy-nilly.

One would hardly care to be the occulists responsible for the well-being of the Cadogan-Craig eyesight. In the magazine field alone, small in print and sometimes pretty niggardly with the ink, they must have read many millions of words. But the sheer volume of the stuff available has not blinded them and they know a good thing when they see it. The publishers of *The Girls' Friend* had no doubt in which social stratum its readers lay and provided gripping yarns called 'Only a Barmaid', 'The Slave of the Shop', 'Madge o' the Mill' and 'Only a Laundry Girl'. There were also 'Winnie, The Workhouse Brat' and, grimly realistic, 'Outcast Effie, or They Made Their Blind Cousin Their Drudge'. Stock school stories were gingered up by the arrival of candid coloured girls, all goggle-eyes and bright ribbons (one of them was a Zulu chief's daughter), together with daredevil Irish colleens endlessly screeching 'begorrah!'

One has, naturally, a favourite moment. This is in one of Dorita Fairlie Bruce's 'Dimsie' books when a plump middle-school girl, anxious to improve her appearance, is caught by the headmistress stripped down to her knickers in school hours but spiritedly ready nevertheless to stand up for her rights: 'There's no school rule that I've ever heard of against trying on new corsets in the lower music-room.'

A WHOLE LOT OF NOTHING

The Times We Had. By Marion Davies (Angus & Robertson, 1976).

The book's sub-title, 'My Life with William Randolph Hearst', tells all.

Marion Davies was a stunningly pretty Ziegfeld Follies girl, a contemporary of Pickles St. Clair, and knew a good thing when she saw it—in this case the vastly rich, powerful, unhappily married newspaper tycoon who bought antiques as though they were the week's groceries and owned San Simeon, possibly the world's largest and most vulgar house.

'Mr. Hearst' was 58 at the time, and Marion was—well, what? She was born in 1897 but was apt to remember the year as 1905. No matter. Diamond wristwatches started to shower down, and she lived with Hearst, unmarried, for the rest of his 32 years. 'Love doesn't need a wedding ring,' she tells us. No indeedy.

Gentlemen prefer, as we know, blondes, and Anita Loos's heroine herself could hardly improve on Miss Davies's prose, which she began to dictate in 1951, the year Hearst died:

> When you're on the stage, you get proposals of marriage, or something. He wanted to make me an honest woman, which was rather ridiculous. When people get married, they get into a lapse of indifference.

San Simeon 'was an awesome thing' and had 60 bedrooms for guests, three butlers, three chefs, 'God knows how many maids'; and the goings-on recorded in *The Times We Had* included visits from a distinguished band of friends, repeatedly thrust into fancy dress for the endless parties.

Mrs. Coolidge got stuck in the elevator: Princess Marie de Bourbon 'fell down and busted the cinema screen'; Ilka Chase complained that 'Mr. Hearst had goosed her in the swimming pool.'

Though Marion was hardly a dedicated film actress ('In silent movies I just had to make faces at the camera'), her gentleman admirer bought her a sort of success in pictures. He minded passionately about her career.

She was, if anything, a comedienne, and threw herself boisterously about, while dialogue was tactfully adjusted for her ('This is a load of crap'), Mr. Hearst constantly urging her to aim higher ('He had wanted me to play Juliet, and I'd practised that a lot'). If things got difficult, 'I put on a pout'.

There were yearly trips abroad with 20 or so guests ('When you went to Europe, you had to understand educationally what the history was'), and all that art in France ('I wanted roller skates so that I could do the Louvre'). But abroad was really a whole lot of nothing:

> That was my impression of Europe. Like when you're hit on the head with a hammer. It feels so good when it stops.

But despite the tastelessness, the appalling waste of time and money, the boozy later years and the general aimlessness, there was an agreeably warm and generous streak in Miss Davies's character (she died in 1961). And, oddly enough, it is clear that she positively loved Mr. Hearst (and he her), and sadly regretted having failed him: 'All my life I wanted to have talent. Finally I had to admit there was nothing there.'

BATTLES OF BRITONS

How We Lived Then. By N. Longmate (Hutchinson, 1971).
He Also Served. By J. Watney (Hamish Hamilton, 1971).

'But what did *you* do in Hitler's War, Granny?' Today's children, mildly interested in our narrow squeak with total disaster, would get some varied replies.

'Well, dear, Grandad was away, waiting to fight, and so I dug for victory and made carrot flan and lentil cutlets and laughed at Lord Haw-Haw and helped with evacuation.'

'What's evacuation?'

'It means moving people to places where they don't want to go and from which they speedily return. Oh, and I extinguished incendiaries and tried not to be a chatter-bug and I queued for offal and whale steaks and in the black-out I repelled advances.'

'Enemy advances?'

'Well, no, they were our own allies, actually.'

'It does sound a funny war, Granny.'

Yes, indeed, funny how odd much of it was (Norman Longmate's factual domestic history, *How We Lived Then*, is superbly detailed and illustrated). Funny funny some of it was, too, as John Watney shows in *He Also Served*, his account of a newly-married second lieutenant trying to find a suitable military niche.

Mr. Watney's hilariously rum experiences, reminiscent of both Waugh and Dad's Army, include being arrested as a spy (a permanent problem, too, for any nun on the move) and trying to insert, at Chequers, an obstreperously rebellious Mr. Churchill into an antique armoured car (it was the only one with a wide enough door).

Later, in the blitz, he had to endure a Middle-European lady giving tongue:

> Thees shelter is kaput. The good German bombs will cut through it like butter. These walls is cardboards. The good

German bombs have delayed fuses. They cut through the walls and then come in here and pouff, we all blow up.

From stirrup pumps to Spam, Mr. Longmate's marvellously comprehensive panorama of the six shattering years misses nothing, and for the middle-aged and elderly, both these excellent books are as evocative as sweet, sad, half-remembered music.

Nothing surprised. A Hammersmith gentleman suggested that a huge raft, cut to the shape of the British Isles, should be floated out into the North Sea to bamboozle bombers.

Patient bus-queuers refused to leave their places even when a V1 cut out overhead. German air losses were reported as though they were cricket scores ('180 for 34') and the coastal telephonic alert for the German invasion was: 'There are fairies at the bottom of your garden.'

THANKS, YANKS

The G.I.s. By Norman Longmate (Hutchinson, 1976).

'They're over-fed, over-sexed, over-paid and over here,' ran a popular anti-American wartime complaint, coupled with 'I don't mind Americans but it's those white fellows they've brought with them.'

Both jibes were, one suspects, invented by envious British troops. The evidence in *The G.I.s*, painstakingly assembled from numerous public and private sources and agreeably presented by an Englishman, Norman Longmate, shows that most civilians felt otherwise.

And suddenly they were here ('We found Yanks all over Ilfracombe'). The first one, Private Milburn H. Henke, setting foot in an Ulster town, affectionately known as Bally-go-Backwards, at the beginning of 1942, and being much fêted, caused only slight embarrassment when it was found that he was of almost pure German descent and had marched ashore beneath ancient bunting which prominently featured the Japanese flag.

There were certainly grounds for envy. The G.I. was about five times better paid than his English counterpart. The uniform was more comfortable. The food and PX (equivalent of N.A.A.F.I.) stores were superb and virtually inexhaustible. Nylons and chocolate helped to ease their providers' way into female hearts. And their chests were already lavishly beribboned (a private, cut by flying glass from a doodle-bug blast, could count on a Purple Heart—a wounded-in-action decoration—in next to no time).

British soldiers were warned what to expect in a pamphlet called 'Meet the Americans' ('Extreme refinement of speech is not admired in male American circles'). Schoolchildren, too, were prepared for the onslaught ('You will get a good mark if you have heard of Babe Ruth, the W. G. Grace of baseball'). But despite this foresight there were muddles, the new arrivals being instantly mistaken for either German parachutists ('Hop it, you!') or Italian prisoners of war.

Our American allies, though educated by the brilliantly compiled 'Short Guide to Great Britain', were similarly baffled and, to cries of 'Holy Cow!' and 'Jeeze!', mistook A.T.S. girls for bus-conductresses, gold-braided cinema commissionaires for Allied generals, and, misled by the absence of railway station nameboards, thought there were towns called HOVIS and BOVRIL.

They were defeated by British money and English slang ('Keep your pecker up'), flinched at our nutritious National Loaf, and became enraged by what was to them the inefficiency of British girl telephone operators ('Say, why don't we parachute them into enemy territory to disrupt communications?').

The mutual ignorance and distrust rapidly vanished. Families absorbed G.I.s as adopted sons. Children clustered round them. Their energy, good nature, high spirits and quite astonishing generosity won most hearts.

They put up with the relative discomfort of Nissen huts and lack of water (it was found that the average American required 75 gallons a day). They drank our warm beer and, miles from home and in a war which was none of their doing, they were prepared to die. What did it matter that they spread marmalade on their fish-cakes? By May, 1944, there were, and thank God, a million and a half of them here. And suddenly they were gone.

Nations seldom feel gratitude, and never love, for another country. But individuals can. These Americans had a rare unselfishness and there was something charmingly naïve about many of them. One remembers a happy occasion when a newly landed and rather ragged body of infantry was being marched in review past an English general. The American colonel leading them felt that an apology was necessary. 'They may not look so hot today, General,' he shouted as they shuffled past, 'but they're a really lovely bunch of boys.'

They were indeed.

IS THIS A RECORD?

HMV *Catalogue* 1914–18. (Republished by David & Charles, 1976).

I've never really cared much about moving with the times. I prefer things to remain exactly as they are. Motor-cars have never been quite the same for me since people stopped winding them up at the front with a handle. In those days, starting the thing was a perpetual problem and challenge. Major Bellamy, keen to take the wife and nippers for a breezy run to the Hog's Back (where Bulldog Drummond, as you'll recall, proposed to Phyllis Benton in comical stage-Irish, a treat that doesn't come every girl's way), would pop on his fawn plus-fours and get to his garage, the home of the family's bullnosed Morris, a full hour before departure time. With Mrs. Bellamy, a pleasing figure in her neat tailor-made and skunk choker, fluttering anxiously to and fro ('Can't you get her going, dear?'), he would flood (whatever that may involve) the carburettor (ditto) and bravely crank his way through a series of loud bangs and explosions. The subsequent chugging through Godalming was done with a real sense of success and achievement and frequently merited a celebration tea at Fuller's, with two goes of walnut layer cake all round.

There were two other things that needed, long ago, to be wound up. Model aeroplanes now work, I gather, on petrol and are radio-controlled but something tells me that it was more fun to twiddle the propeller while strands of black bunjie coiled and writhed and double- and treble-knotted until one dared twiddle no further. Then came the launch into the wind, the soaring flight over the laburnum, and the nose-dive into the next garden and poor Mrs. Spence's red-hot pokers, whence it had to be constantly retrieved ('Ask her *very* nicely, now'). But best of all the windings, and even now I miss doing it, were those necessary for gramophones.

In childhood my great friends were Joan and 'Boysie' (I never knew any other name) Brimblecombe and their Barnes nursery contained a priceless object. It was wartime, Great Wartime, and their Uncle Hubert had not only gone courageously down to the sea in a ship but under the sea as well in a submarine (he had, I hasten to say, come up again). He used to take with him, and it must have been a very early model, his portable gramophone (can it have been a Decca?), doubtless hoping to play it while submerged, but there was a snag. The Navy was fearful that Clara Butt's majestic chest-notes, given fullest play in 'My ain folk', might reverberate through the water, a fine sound conductor, and reach the ears of old Jerry, slyly lurking silently on the sea-bed nearby. So Uncle Hubert had had to abandon music and had kindly passed on this cherished instrument to his niece and nephew, together with a splendidly large pile of records, and all day long we cranked and played and cranked and played.

We took it in turns to choose a record. Joan had just begun dancing lessons and was especially fond of a tuneful piece called 'Dance of the Disappointed Fairies'. Second time round she would plump for 'The Tickle Toe' or 'The Glow-Worm Idyll' with, in reserve, musical tributes to our gallant allies—'Dance of Ivan Ivanovitch', 'Valse poudrée' and 'Marche Italienne' (a bit unspirited, though we didn't realise it then, and even a bit backwards at Caporetto). When not in dancing mood, she tended to go for one of the single-sided violet celebrity discs which were expensive (7s) but brought such rich joys as honey-voiced Alma Gluck requesting to be carried back to old Virginny. There was also what must, I think, have been one of the Woodforde-Finden Indian love lyrics entitled 'On Jhelum River—Ashoo at her Lattice', known to us, we were very young, as Atishoo at her Lattice.

Boysie was more robust and belligerent and was, as indeed we all were, firmly anti-German and for him there was quite a choice. There was a humorous talking record called 'The Kaiser on the Telephone'. There were 'I'm the great big pot of Potsdam', 'Who bashed Bill Kaiser?' and 'The Hindenburg Trot'. He particularly enjoyed 'Belgium put the Khibosh on the Kaiser', historically an extremely doubtful claim, and the rattling choruses of bouncy Harry Dearth:

Of course you know I'm Gipsy Joe,
Ha, ha, ha! Ho, ho, ho!

All these records are now referred to as 'the old 78s', not always correctly. Some indeed were 78 rpm but the recommended revolutions per minute varied and you had to keep alert and continually adjust the speed-regulator. Kreisler's 'Berceuse' and John McCormack's 'Mother o'mine' revolved at a sober 77. 'Angels guard thee' (sung in Russian) required a feeble 75. Things hotted up for the Peer Gynt Suite, 'In the Hall of the Mountain King' whirling round at 82, while the fastest clip of the lot, 88 if you please, was for 'Shipmates o'mine'.

I am afraid that I, irresponsible as ever, chose records that were, to me, pleasingly dotty. There were two songs, 'Where did Robinson Crusoe go with Friday on Saturday Night?' and 'What ho! Mr. Watteau', that had me in stitches. There were also endless numbers that had agreeably jiggy tunes but which meant very little: 'Yacka Hula Hickey Dula', 'Yaddie Kaddie Kiddie Kaddie Koo' and 'Oh how she could Yacki Hacki Wickie Wacki Woo'. And for careful memorising and subsequent rendering in my own nursery, until shushed, there were 'Cut me off a little bit of roly-poly' and 'Auntie Skinner's Chicken Dinner'.

For such a recent invention, the range of record was very wide and, interspersed with all this jollity, there were thoughtful moments. There was Dr. Grenfell, C.M.G., 'Adrift on an ice-floe', a year or so before Lilian Gish in *Way Down East*. Commander Peary was to be heard discovering the North Pole and Sir E. Shackleton led a 'Dash for the South Pole'. There were three, heaven help us, budget speeches (Asquith, Lloyd George and Churchill). British troops passed through Boulogne (clump, clump, to martial music) and a captive nightingale sadly warbled. And from the Cadbury Model Village came 'the finest carillon in Britain'—'The Bells o'Bournville'.

But how, you wonder, do I remember all this? I don't. Most of the nursery pieces are with me still in memory's echoing chambers, but otherwise I am lucky to have before me, reprinted at £5.25, an HMV Catalogue for 1914–1918. And what publishing firm would nobly venture on such an esoteric subject? David & Charles, of course, of Newton Abbot, public benefactors. If your interests happen to lie in left-handed railway guards with ginger hair who worked on the L.N.E.R. in 1922, David & Charles have probably produced a book about them.

MORE GOOD THAN HARM

Very Superior Men. By Alicia C. Percival (Charles Knight, 1973).
The Public Schools. By Brian Gardner (Hamish Hamilton, 1973).

Those who hated their public school days (and which literary gent would ever dare to say he had had a whale of a time?) can meet in Alicia C. Percival's admirable *Very Superior Men* some of the architects of their discomfitures.

Miss Percival's title was Thring of Uppingham's opinion of those attending the first Headmasters' Conference in 1869. It was the time when, the day of the private tutor having passed, many public schools were struggling to raise their numbers from 50 to 500, and gradually succeeding.

The Conference's predecessors had been vigorous and grim. A snap of the Shrewsbury staff of 1856 shows only one smiling face—a gnome-like usher (geography and woodwork?) who has plainly just been dismissed.

There was Dr. Busby of Westminster, an ardent flogger, and a Gillray cartoon in Brian Gardner's *The Public Schools* shows him whacking away at bare bottoms with spare birches at the ready. There was Keate of Eton, who absentmindedly thrashed all the Confirmation candidates queueing up outside his door for comfortable words.

There was Butler of Shrewsbury who expelled all his prefects for complaining about the beef. There was Pears of Repton who, after his first visit to inspect the school, sat slumped forward, gently moaning. There was Welldon of Tonbridge (early runs and cold baths). And, bristling with manliness and piety, there was Arnold of Rugby.

On the memorial tablet to Grignon of Felsted were the words ONE SOWETH, ANOTHER REAPETH, and by and large, as Mr. Gardner's excellently researched history shows, they sowed more good than harm. The best ones (among them, Thring, Sanderson of Oundle and Roxburgh of Stowe) were warm-hearted and dedicated fanatics with instant built-in communication with boys, Sanderson bravely leading the way into the scientific 20th century.

Resentments still, naturally, exist. Mr. Gardner quotes a Labour M.P. as saying:

> Never be deceived that one buys a better education; one buys advantage and a privileged position in society; that is what the public school system is all about.

Examination results, which are really all we have to go on, make nonsense of this cobwebby view. It may not be 'fair' to be able to buy a better education, but it is unwise to try to twist the facts (Mr. Gardner's Tables of Success are very revealing).

Some splendid oddities have been unearthed. Henry VI gave Eton the sites of Leicester Square, Piccadilly and most of Mayfair, and Henry VIII, as was his wont, took them back again. There was the Harrow revolt of 1808 when the boys barricaded the London Road and seized the keys of the birch cupboard.

There was the Marlborough rebellion of 1851 (juniors were being branded on the forearm). There was famine at Radley in 1853, the inmates eagerly munching flowers, bulbs and acorns. And how delightful to discover that Malvern partly owes its foundation to the understandable and well-merited popularity of Lea and Perrin's Worcestershire sauce.

ABSOLUTELY HELPLESS WITH MIRTH

Berry & Co., Jonah & Co., Adele & Co. By Dornford Yates (Ward Lock, 1976).

Behind the box hedges of the rose gardens, tall elms and copper beeches can be seen. Beyond the ha-ha, rolling parkland stretches. In the stable yard a Rolls stands ready, waiting for Fitch, the chauffeur, to make it purr into action. In the distance the bells of Bilberry church ring out their summons to worship.

Know where we are? You will soon enough, for within the vast house (staff of 15) can be heard wild 'peals of merriment' and 'refreshing gurgles', with everybody 'helpless with mirth'.

They've now been helpless for many years. We are at White Ladies in the New Forest area of Hampshire and in the rib-tickling presence of Dornford Yates's most memorable creations, Berry Pleydell, his wife, Daphne, her brother, Boy, and their cousins Jonah and Jill, making five first cousins in all, living permanently together in what some might regard as an almost incestuous relationship.

But they don't waste all their time merrily chuckling at White Ladies. There is Mayfair for the season and another fully-staffed house, with polo and golf at Ranelagh, top hats and strolls down Bond Street, beanos at Brooks's, shopping at Fortnum's, or quiet evenings at home and the butler, Falcon, hovering with caviare sandwiches.

And everywhere there is Berry, a perfect scream (starting young, he was rated a wit at Harrow) with a repertoire of jokes:

'Are you fond of kidneys?'
'Passionately. I used to gather them as a child.'

What on earth would modern teenagers make of it all? Older

readers will blink and blink again to realise with what delight they in their youth lapped the luxurious stuff up.

Those with firm stomachs can now lap again after the reprinting of 'Berry & Co.', 'Jonah & Co.' and 'Adele & Co.', which the publishers have re-issued in response to a continual stream of letters from fans unable to obtain original copies.

Dornford Yates, who looked like a handsome, moustachioed cross between Sapper and John Buchan, was born in 1885 and educated at Harrow and Oxford, where he was president of the O.U.D.S. He practised at the bar, assisting in the downfall of Crippen; his Berry stories and the Pleydell family, whose lives contain so much of that of Yates himself, first appeared in 1911, and his first major success, 'Berry & Co.', in 1920.

After that, however, the author had no time for England: he went to live in France, where he built himself a series of villas, and then in 1940 moved via Portugal to Rhodesia, where he remained until his death in 1960.

Nobody has summed up the particular appeal of the Berry series better than John Betjeman: 'They are the pipe-dreams and Black Magic chocolate hopes of all middle-class folk.' The books formed the backbone of between-the-wars, escapist, wish-fulfilment literature (how *smart* we all felt), and they went with the novels of Buchan and Sapper.

These three authors are dissimilar in many ways and in none more so than in humour. If there is any in Buchan, I have, alas, missed it. In Sapper it is limited to Hugh Drummond's and his cronies' schoolboyish quips. But in Dornford Yates it is ceaseless and nowadays seems about as amusing as a weekend with Stalin.

Never mind: there are the girls, always all of a piece—dimpled, stunningly pretty, standing frequently 'a-tiptoe' and often 'the pink of daintiness'. They are ready for endless saucy chatter and any reputable jape ('Eagerness danced from her eyes, energy leapt from her carriage'). They tend to wear 'kimonos of softest apricot' and to have unusual names: Maisie Dukedom, Estelle de Swete, Lady Sue Fustian, Mona Deodore, Madrigal Stukeley.

And best of all, nobody at any point does a stroke of work. Where the cash comes from, we are not told. We only know where it doesn't, in any full measure, go: to cooks ('Surely the breed can't be extinct') or gnarled road-menders ('He pulled a forelock with the antique courtesy of his class'). In general, Berry & Co. are scornful of anybody outside their own circle, in particular foreigners, people holding liberal views, and Hebrews.

Sometimes the stories become dramatic, and for this the text flashes excitingly into italics. Sometimes the 'convulsions' of merriment stop, and, with a noisy gear-change, we find ourselves bogged down in a purple patch ('A pride of clouds rode high in heaven', etc.)

Heart-warming stuff! But for me it is still Buchan first, Sapper a splendid second, and the rest—including Dornford Yates—some way behind.

GREAT SHEIK-UP

Bestseller. By Claud Cockburn (Sidgwick & Jackson, 1972).

How odd that such an arid substance as sand should have sparked off some of the century's best-selling romances.

You certainly never knew who you were going to bump into in the desert. Coming unexpectedly round a dune, you might find 'The Sheik' making a beast of himself with proud Diana Mayo:

> Proud Diana Mayo had the history of her race at her fingers' ends and gloried in the long line of upright men and chaste women.

'Upright' hardly describes her treatment at the Sheik's dusky hands. One minute the mettlesome girl finds herself hurled athwart a saddle and galloped away with, and the next she is thrust through a tent-flap, spreadeagled on a camp (presumably) bed, and repeatedly interfered with.

A few miles away, tempestuous Domini Enfilden is to be seen, gazing out over the sandy plains (locally known as 'the Garden of Allah'), her nostrils wildly working:

> She wanted the bloomy purple nights, the roar of the tom-toms, the clash of the cymbals, the rattle of the negroes' castanets.

What she actually gets is a lapsed Trappist with no visible castanets but who comes pleasingly up to scratch under canvas.

Or over there on the horizon, sturdily tramping along with the Legion, is gallant 'Beau Geste', firmly caught in the most improbable story every penned and landed with an outstandingly silly name:

> 'Don't you see, darling, he's a "beau" Geste who makes a *beau geste.*'
> 'Oh I say, that's damned ingenious.'

Sand, too, wove its magic spell in 'The Blue Lagoon', where the shipwrecked cousins, Dick and Emmeline, abandon their desert-island disc in favour of non-musical activities. This was just the kind of book which, if the author's luck was in, the then Bishop of London, dear wonky old Winnington-Ingram, would condemn from the pulpit, thus ensuring lively sales.

In *Bestseller* ('The Books That Everyone Read: 1900–1939'), Claud Cockburn guides us with relish through this weird literature. He misses none of the fun, nor the sociological implications of much that went on, though he doesn't make heavy weather of his researches and lets the enjoyable stuff speak for itself.

Like many another, Mr. Cockburn has no great opinion of the 1920s and 1930s:

> It may well be that in a better world many of the best-sellers would have been seen as superfluous or even contemptible. But things being what they were they did, at worst, produce a good grade of opium.

How important for some it was in those sad and rather idiotic days to have read these things ('Do remind me, Hilda, to change my book at Boots') Middle-class people dining out were wise to have under their belts, in addition to the obligatory grapefruit, whitebait and cutlets, the precise reason why 'Boy' Fenwick, husband of Iris Storm (who wore 'The Green Hat') plunged to his death from a Deauville balcony on the wedding-night (he thought he'd got you-know-what).

One can't, of course, have everything, and if one's own favourites ('Tell England' and 'The Rosary') are missing from Mr. Cockburn's survey, who can complain when room has been found for so much else—'The Broad Highway', 'Sorrell and Son', and, in particular, 'If Winter Comes'.

Strange to think that if only its heroine, Nona, Lady Tybar, had had the telephone installed at her great mansion, Northropps, many of the wintry tribulations that came Mark Sabre's way need never ('I am trying to connect you') have come at all.

SHE'S A LADY

A Night to Remember. By Walter Lord.
The Liners. By Terry Coleman (both Allen Lane, 1976).

I possess a Christian name that has seen better days. It is not now quite as outlandish as, say, Archibald or Adolphus or Hildebrand would be, but it's as much of a has-been as Vernon and Hubert and Oswald. Doting modern parents, wavering excitedly over the choice between Giles and Simon (brother for Samantha Jane), would not give Arthur a single thought. Its decline was sadly sudden. Perfectly O.K., and even quite *distingué* when allied to Connaught, up to and including the first world war, it speedily became in the 20s a name that writers of fiction allotted to tipsy commercial travellers and bovine buffers ('Good old Arthur!'). I first became aware at school that all was not well when I had to spout it out, for some exam registration reason, in class: sniggers from the safe set of Johns, Davids and Michaels. That pleasingly eccentric ITV cat which advertised some pussy food or other by inserting its left leg into the tin and scooping out pawfuls of deliciousness was called, I need hardly say, Arthur. Oh well.

When, on a trip by boat to Canada in 1970, I presented, as instructed, my relatively recent passport to the purser and his face fell, I assumed that it was the name that had upset him. It could hardly have been the photographic likeness of my top half, all too accurate, as he had already been feasting his eyes on the real thing during our preliminary chat. But there were my names and my 'Description' written out, as requested, in capital letters in my own hand—eyes 'hazel', hair 'grey', which it then was—and with them the entry for 'Profession'. Here there had been a problem. Since abandoning schoolmastering, I had correctly made use, at different periods, of 'Secretary' and 'Script

Editor'. But what now? I have already dealt in these columns with the possibilities, or impossibilities, of 'Belle Lettriste'. 'Freelance' has undesirable military connections, and 'Literator' is high-falutin. So, for this passport, I had settled on the simple word, WRITER, and then I saw what had troubled the purser. I had imperfectly formed the first R and the profession I was claiming was seen to be that of 'WAITER'. As a calling, waiter was clearly not tippy-top on the purser's list of preferences. This, coupled with a voice that can only be described as hoity-toity, had convinced him that I was some sort of impostor.

But apart from this little set-back, everything else on that agreeable Empress boat was *couleur de rose*. 'The Liner she's a lady' wrote Kipling, and though I fancy he meant it slightly disparagingly in comparison with harder-working little cargo-boats, nothing could have been more graceful or gentle than our passage. How mad of the world to allow this charming method of travel to dwindle away. The most animated passengers on board were a group of delightful, cherry-cheeked nuns who, though voluminously dressed throughout, whizzed about at deck quoits and shuffleboard, rushed headlong into every film showing or game of bingo and at mealtimes munched like mad. Their order evidently forbade strong waters but they pressed their noses flat against the windows of bars and sipped mentally.

Somewhere near Newfoundland, a sizeable iceberg was sighted on the horizon and the ship's wag made a series of tasteless jokes (we cold-shouldered him at dinner) about the Titanic and Davy Jones's locker. In the power that that dreadful event still has to fascinate and horrify, the Titanic is unsinkable indeed. How right Mrs. Ledoux had been, in her 'Ocean Notes for Ladies', to stress the importance for female voyagers of dressing well at all times as a body washed ashore in good clothing always received more courteous treatment. There is, across the years, a splendidly opulent and well-dressed ring to some of the names—Mrs. Washington Dodge, Mrs. Dickinson Bishop, Mrs. J. C. Hogeboom and Mrs. Charlotte Cardoza, who travelled with 38 feather boas and 91 pairs of gloves. A first-class ticket on the Titanic proved a prudent expenditure, a much higher proportion of both ladies and gentlemen being mercifully saved than in steerage, and besides, on that 'night to remember' (Allen Lane has just reissued, illustrated and at £4.95, Walter Lord's masterpiece, together with a splendidly nostalgic *The Liners* by Terry Coleman, at £5.95), there was an excellent dinner of consommé Olga, asparagus vinaigrette, mousseline of salmon and Waldorf Pudding. For the second class there was consommé tapioca, and baked haddock. What was offered in steerage we do not know. Full of salmon, Lady Duff Gordon kept her cool in the very sparsely occupied lifeboat No. 1, remarking to her secretary, Miss Francatelli, as the icy waters closed over the liner, 'There is your beautiful nightdress gone'. And the lives of 1502 people with it.

One goggles afresh at the extraordinary facts. The look-out who spotted, too late, the iceberg had no binoculars (he had asked for them but was told that there were none available). For a full hour, the look-out in the stern was unaware that anything was amiss. There was a curious tendency for hopeful escapees to stuff their pockets with oranges. The ship's telegraphic code contained the useful words BACK (baggage gone astray) and RAPIDO (sinking rapidly). There was the unaccountably static behaviour of those on the *Californian*, halted eight miles away, who watched a large, stationary liner firing rockets, then appearing to tilt, then disappearing. And there was the Titanic investigation committee, who really covered just about everything, even going thoughtfully into the question of what an iceberg was actually composed of. 'Ice', somebody suggested.

We owe much to Mr. Coleman, in particular the warning that when at sea, bishops are apt to become very undisciplined, and also the information that there exists (in America, natch) a Society of Titanic Enthusiasts, 300 strong. In 1972, on the 60th anniversary of the disaster, they went to town and managed to dig up, so to speak, and fête seven ancient survivors ('these living, fine, historical people'). They arranged for a wreath to be laid on the sea at the very spot and, on a pond nearer home, built a four foot radio-directed model of the Titanic and a suitably-sized papier mâché iceberg, hoping that the two would manage to collide and excitingly re-enact the little misfortune. No such luck, however, so the ship had to be scuttled by remote control. Elsewhere, some of the Enthusiasts gave a 'fun party' on two lifeboats labelled Titanic. 'Boat drill scheduled to start at eight o'clock', said the invitations, '1912 attire required.' One can only assume that the Society's president is Charles Addams.

HARD MATTRESSES

The Best of British Pluck. By Philip Warner (Macdonald and Jane's, 1976).

Some Hull schoolchildren, examined recently on their knowledge of the last war and of Hitler, replied that he had a toothbrush moustache, made a lot of rather loud speeches and invented a political party called the Nancies. Well, yes and no. The Hull pupils did, in my view, rather well. In similar circumstances some sixty years ago one would oneself have fared a bit ignominiously. I knew, of course, about the Kaiser, all bristles and ferocity, who was going to hang everybody from lamp-posts. Then there were those remarkable Bernard Partridge cartoons in *Punch*, a weekly treat which often depicted, against a shell-torn background, poor Peace, with the back of one hand across her eyes to shut out the horrid sights and sheltering plucky little Belgium in the folds of her robe, while in the foreground was to be seen a sturdy, female France, wearing a Napoleonic hat and apron and sensible clogs, holding out a grateful hand across the channel to a prosperous-looking John Bull and saying something like '*Merci, mon brave!*'. A likely story. Further wartime information of a highly-coloured and doubtfully reliable kind came to me from a popular sort of fiction for boys, the rattling good yarns of Percy F. Westerman, author of *A Lively Bit of the Front*. From them one discovered that when not actually at the Front and in uniform, all German men were in England and imperfectly disguised as spies (you could tell them from their 'shuffling gait'), were apt to mutter '*Himmel!*' and '*Donnerwetter!*' when under pressure and were invariably unkind to animals, especially dogs. Could Hunnish conduct go further?

Mr. Westerman's rattling yarns appeared in the *Boy's Own Paper* (always known to its readers as the B.O.P.), a monthly magazine with an entirely wholesome tone (it was published under the wing of the Religious Tract Society) and chock-a-block with useful information on varied subjects. One learnt 'How to apply for a position as a lighthousekeeper', 'How to boil water in a paper bag', 'How to make an electric trumpet', 'What to do with addled hawks' eggs', 'How to catch ostriches' (put on an ostrich feather hood and so 'hoodwink' them, ha ha), 'How to stuff reptiles', 'How to make birdlime' (boil mistletoe berries to destruction) and 'How to keep spiders as pets'. There was a stirring article on 'How I swam the channel' by Captain Webb ('I rubbed myself all over with porpoise oil, dived in and struck out for Cap Gris Nez'), the gallant captain getting sharply stung by jelly-fish (French ones, doubtless) and wading ashore to the strains of 'Rule Britannia'. Though there was no article actually called 'How not to get into bad habits', the fear of you-know-what was everywhere expressed in feverish editorials. Take cold baths, sleep on a hard mattress, fling wide the windows, exercise vigorously with dumb-bells, turn in dog tired, eat sparingly ('Fat makes duffers') and, if 'troubled' by sexual thoughts, on no account visit an art gallery. With a final warning about noses falling off, blindness, nervous twitches, insanity, the mad-house and suicide, we could pass on to less fussing matters such as what to do for the best with chilblains, bunions and blackheads.

We owe all these delightful facts to a senior lecturer at Sandhurst, Philip Warner, who, enthusiastically burrowing about in the back numbers, has produced, in *The Best of British Pluck*, a splendid selection of B.O.P. articles, stories and illustrations from the 88 years of its life, and a perceptive and admiring introduction (and a sense of humour) to go with it.

But despite all the care and attention lavished on the readers, the 'Answers to Correspondents' usually finds the editor in a somewhat crisp mood. 'No one with your handwriting could hope to get a job in a bank' is hardly encouraging. 'Spots on the forehead' is told 'Your blood is impure. Do you study to keep holy in thought by day?'. A keen apiarist gets a rap over the knuckles ('How do you expect us to name a bumble bee which has been squashed flat in the post?'). Though some readers are, as usual, more equal than others ('Glandular scars will prevent you from being accepted for the Marines unless as an officer'), the editor's intention, when the magazine first began as a weekly in 1879, was to appeal to all classes, and he sold it at the accessible price of 1d. It was perfectly normal to find a school article on Winchester alongside a description, fully illustrated, of the new Working Lads Institute in Whitechapel, or an account of an exciting mutiny at Eton (they threw eggs at the Provost) cheek by jowl with life on the Humber Training Ship at Southampton. Indeed, working lads were a prime consideration and, after Dr. W. G. Grace has given some brisk hints on cricket ('Hold the bat firmly and don't twirl it about') and we have gazed at snaps of whiskery boat race crews, the lads are reminded of the perils of gin palaces and music halls ('the dancing is disgusting') and of other dangers (hard mattresses again) and are told that the fact that they have to be at the factory gates at 6 a.m. is no excuse for skipping cold baths.

In the B.O.P. there was, for some tastes, rather too much emphasis on physical punishments in general and beating in particular. There are articles such as 'Under the Rod' and 'Swishing Anecdotes' from the fertile pen of 'Cuthbert Bede'. Elsewhere we find 'Famous Floggers' (who was the headmaster who absent-mindedly caned six boys waiting outside his study, forgetting that they were intending confirmands who had come to hear him discourse on 'The meaning of the spirit'?). The description of the assembling, twig by twig, of a birch leads one to suspect that there was somebody in the editorial office who had a problem.

Most important of all and wonderfully good were the serialised adventure stories, and in choosing their authors (among them, Jules Verne, Henty, Conan Doyle, Algernon Blackwood) the editors knew their business. How thrilling it used to be, reading away safe and snug and warm in bed, to be marooned on an ice floe, to come face to face with a Bengal tiger, to struggle with the sharks of Mauritius, or to fall off a cliff locked in a grizzly's hairy embrace, its hot breath on one's face and its great slavering jaws (see illustration) an inch from one's nose.

HIS MASTER'S VOICE

The Life of Noël Coward. By Cole Lesley (Cape, 1976).

When J. B. Priestley, rather late in the day (it was 1964) put his jocular question to Noël Coward, 'What is all this nonsense about you being called the Master?', the answer, in that widely imitated and highly individual voice was 'It started as a joke and became true.' After a first meeting with Noël in 1930, T. E. Lawrence wrote humourlessly but fairly accurately to Mrs. G. B. Shaw, 'He is not deep but remarkable. A hasty kind of genius. I wonder what his origin is?' Previous biographers of the Master, a name by no means nonsensical to everybody, have been well intentioned but inadequate, providing little more than a re-hash of his own *Present Indicative* and *Future Indefinite*, filled out by that deadliest of materials, old press cuttings. Cole Lesley, secretary, companion and friend to Sir Noël for forty years, makes no such mistakes. 'I want you to tell the truth,' Noël said when discussing with him his possible future role as biographer. He has done just that, and with a charm and tact reminiscent of those shown by Daphne du Maurier when writing about her famous father in *Gerald*. Mr. Lesley displays, in this first book, quite unusual gifts and if there has been a better or more fascinating theatrical biography in the last fifty years, it has not come my way.

For one joyous thing in these dim days, one laughs aloud, and with Noël *fou rire* and hysteria were ever just round the corner. There was a hearty English major who, blushingly confessing that he was 'a bit of a poet', thrust into Noël's hand some verses which ended

> Oh simple shepherd, praise thy God
> That thou art nothing but a sod.

There were the esoteric bits of information fed to him by the distinguished historian, Hester Chapman: 'It is now incontrovertibly proved that Queen Boadicea is buried beneath platform eleven at St. Pancras.' All his life, he found certain names (Budleigh Salterton, Uckfield) irresistibly comical. In youth, he took part, as a peculiarly mobile mushroom, in an *Autumn Idyll* ballet with a petite *danseuse* called Saza Puttfarcken. He 'walked on' occasionally in that splendidly stagey piece, *The Best of Luck*, at Drury Lane and for years after would declaim dramatically at odd moments, 'May God forgive you, Blanche Westermere, for I never shall.' Travelling in Europe with Cochran to find a suitable leading man for *Bitter Sweet*, they discovered in Vienna a handsome young tenor and, on asking his name, found it to be Hans Unterfucker: so they settled for George Metaxa instead. Wild laughter, that rare pleasure, is common among actors. Even Sir Laurence himself was once, we learn, nearly expelled from the Birmingham Rep for giggling.

Best of all perhaps (and here, though facts are facts, I must ask sensitive readers to bear with us or to skip the paragraph) were the unconscious verbal bricks dropped by the charming and handsome writer, painter and sculptor, Winifred Clemence Dane, large and impressive in her flowing gowns ('Do come to dinner', she used to boom down the telephone, 'I've got a nice cock'). Totally innocent and unworldly, she settled, as though by magic, on the one unfortunate word ('Olwen's got crabs!' she cried excitedly to guests arriving for a wartime lunch). She stayed with Binkie Beaumont in the country ('Oh the pleasure of waking up to see a row of tits outside your window!'), and a kind friend had to explain to her that she simply could not say in her latest novel, 'He stretched out and grasped the other's gnarled, stumpy tool.' To the pure all things are pure but there were anxious moments when Noël, keen to learn how to sculpt, came to her studio for a lesson. 'Noël, dear boy, you must wipe your tool. You cannot work with a dirty tool. Now then, stick it right up and work away, either from the front or the back, whichever comes easiest.' Going to the Old Vic on a hot summer's evening in a taxi with Joyce Carey, Winifred was bellowing on about the ancient subject of whether Bacon had written Shakespeare, summing up her view that Bacon was merely Shakespeare's informant in tones audible for miles around: 'Yes, I have no doubt that Shakespeare sucked Bacon dry and that Bacon very much liked being sucked.' Miss Carey, mindful of the driver's susceptibilities and fearful of what infelicities there might be still to come, leant forward and hastily shut the open glass window between them.

Mr. Lesley has been able to draw on a mass of new material—letters, diaries, journals, friends' memories and an invaluable object called 'Mum's suitcase' in which Mrs. Coward kept any scrap of paper which had a bearing on her adored and brilliantly precocious son ('He was very forward and amusing...a most attractive child, never a bit shy'). But alas, it was not for nothing that she shared a birthday with Hitler. Though in his letters to her she was 'Darling old Mummysnooks' or 'Ducky old Diddleums', she did not deceive him ('Mum really was a wicked old devil, wasn't she?') with her possessiveness, selfishness and her ability to brew up family rows. A hint of her quality is to be seen when she gazed down at her dead sister, Vida, in her coffin: 'Doesn't she look pretty, like a little snowdrop. It's a pity she looked so disagreeable when she was alive.' Mr. Coward senior was a rather pathetic and frequently unemployed musical nonentity whose only claims to fame were to have fathered Noël and to have a sister locally known as 'The Twickenham Nightingale'. Formidable and determined mothers are by no means unknown in the theatre: after all, we owe the Marx Brothers entirely to a Jewish momma. Mr. Lesley is hilarious on one of the most famous, Clifton Webb's dreaded Mabelle, a doting mother who required a daily dozen or so dry martinis to keep her going and who had the really very weird distinction of having combed the dead Rudolph Valentino's hair into the correct position before he could be displayed to his fans. When Mabelle died, completely gaga and 94, Clifton Webb cried for two months. Noël rang him up ('Unless you stop blubbing I shall reverse the charges') adding, as he rang off, 'It must be extremely tough to be orphaned at the age of seventy-one.'

Everything is here in fullest detail and with numerous and splendid photographs—the dazzling career ('Destiny's Tot' Alexander Woollcott called him), the astounding social success ('I am sick to death of having quiet suppers with the King and Mrs. Simpson'), the golden years of 1928 to 1934 and of *This Year of Grace*, *Cavalcade* and *Bitter Sweet* (its triumphant American opening was in New York during the Wall Street crash, and its author wrote 'Evelyn Laye is weeing down her leg with excitement and people are hurling themselves off buildings like confetti'). Through it all, his politeness to the public was impeccable ('As long as there are people who wait for my autograph, I shall give it') and, contrary to the general view, it was perfectly simple pleasures ('The life of the very rich is not for me') that pleased him most—evenings with old friends and old jokes, some music, 'a little eggy something on a tray' and a nice early bed with E. Nesbit or Saki.

Everywhere the famous snap judgments are rattled out. Chamberlain ('You can't trust a man whose neck is too thin for his collar'). Mozart ('It sounds like somebody piddling on wet flannel'). Mary Baker Eddy ('I suppose she's been responsible for more deaths than anyone except Hitler'). Modern painters ('One sees a square lady with three breasts and a guitar up her crotch'). A wider education, and there had been virtually none at all, might have brought some more balanced and generous views, but his knowledge of human nature was instinctive and profound and when the sad and unpopular days came, he was in no way surprised ('I am being made to pay for all my years of success').

Cole Lesley has been faithful to his instructions about telling the truth, not that there is a great deal on the debit side. Noël was bossy and liked his own way. He flew into violent rages about nothing, wailing 'Life deals me blow after blow.' When he fell in love (and for those who like to know such things, it was with chaps), his sense of humour vanished completely. He could be very sharp with people. Though entirely unjealous about the success of others, he was extremely selfish. It's not, as you see, much of a list, and there is such a lot, in addition to the enormous pleasure he gave in the theatre and elsewhere, on the credit side. Nobody put up more politely or heroically with bores. Nobody encouraged true talent more. And, above all, he made everybody laugh. Who but he would have said, after reading Monica Baldwin's *I Leap Over the Wall*, 'It has strengthened me in my decision not to become a nun.'